# DARK WAVES

# POPULAR MUSICS MATTER: SOCIAL, POLITICAL AND CULTURAL INTERVENTIONS

**Series Editors:** *Eoin Devereux, Aileen Dillane and Martin J. Power*

The Popular Musics Matter: Social, Political and Cultural Interventions series will publish internationally informed edited collections, monographs and textbooks that engage in the critical study of popular music performance (live and recorded), historical and contemporary popular music practitioners and artists, and participants and audiences for whom such musics embody aesthetic, cultural, and, particularly, socio-political values. The series sees music not only as a manifestation of global popular culture but also as a form that profoundly shapes and continually seeks to redefine our understandings of how society operates in a given location and era.

### Titles in the Series

# DARK WAVES

## The Synthesizer and the Dystopian Sound of Britain (1977–80)

NEIL O'CONNOR

ROWMAN & LITTLEFIELD
*Lanham • Boulder • New York • London*

Published by Rowman & Littlefield
An imprint of The Rowman & Littlefield Publishing Group, Inc.
4501 Forbes Boulevard, Suite 200, Lanham, Maryland 20706
www.rowman.com

86-90 Paul Street, London EC2A 4NE

British Library Cataloguing in Publication Information Available

**Library of Congress Cataloging-in-Publication Data**

Names: O'Connor, Neil, 1979- author.
Title: Dark waves : the synthesizer and the dystopian sound of Britain
   (1977-80) / Neil O'Connor.
Description: Lanham : Rowman & Littlefield Publishers, 2023. | Series:
   Popular musics matter: social, political and cultural interventions |
   Includes bibliographical references and index.
Identifiers: LCCN 2022052199 (print) | LCCN 2022052200 (ebook) |
   ISBN 9781538165300 (cloth) | ISBN 9781538165317 (epub)
Subjects: LCSH: Electronica (Music)--Great Britain--History and criticism.
   | Popular music--Great Britain--1971-1980--History and criticism. |
   Synthesizer (Musical instrument)--Great Britain--History.
Classification: LCC ML3492 .O26 2023 (print) | LCC ML3492 (ebook) |
   DDC 781.6480941/09047--dc23/eng/20221130
LC record available at https://lccn.loc.gov/2022052199
LC ebook record available at https://lccn.loc.gov/2022052200

# CONTENTS

# FOREWORD

I stepped into the seventh decade of the twentieth century on a day of personal significance—the first of January 1970, my fifteenth birthday. An age that suggests the ensuing trauma of adulthood, but with the optimism and uncertainty of youth still ringing loudly through me. In a wider world, it was also the dawn of a decade that similarly carried both the residual disruption of the previous years, matched with not-unreasonable expectations. The horrors of the Vietnam War, widespread civil unrest, and shifting geopolitical tectonic plates were frequently masked by the promise of new technologies and Technicolor media, all driven by the boom of movement and voracious consumerism. It was a decade of first-world acceleration and the resulting disorder of global entropy. The year itself was largely uneventful, but the seventies and the early years of the eighties proved to be a period of unpredictable change. A time in which future dreams were made corporeal against the backdrop of economic, social, and technological transformation, and importantly, a time captured most vividly through the exploding spectacle of popular culture.

The period marked a wider sense of growing up, of post-war reality that had been put on hold by a sixties naïve euphoria reluctant to address its systemic complexities. On a national level, the pressures played out in a dysfunctional political landscape, struck by inertia in dealing with a sclerotic, largely nineteenth-century industrial infrastructure, shaped by class, race, and regional divisions. Successive governments neglected the reality of post-war migration and merely inflamed racial tensions whilst the notion of a growing moneyed, urbane, service industry was at odds with a fractious working class.

The cutting adrift of the industrial North did not start with the current neo-Tory, levelling up, red-wall political zeitgeist. I grew up in

Sheffield, the frontline of this very real divide. The People's Republic of South Yorkshire. A city built on the monoculture of steel, buttressed by the coalfields of the surrounding areas. An area of general classlessness, in the sense that everyone readily identified as 'working class,' but also one that, after the disruption of war, blind to changing global economics, saw its future through a vision of a potential shiny future. 'Sheffield: City of the Future' boldly sold itself to the world. A booming youth who saw a new world of television, music, and life-changing technology. The darkness illuminated by the bright lights of the actually-realised space age. This clash between emotions and reality encapsulated both personal experiences and the events in the real world. We saw this flashing, push-button destiny alongside rubbish-strewn streets, power cuts, and industrial action.

The perception that electronic music, this emergent form slowly encroaching the growing music world during the second half of the seventies, was driven by an avalanche of Japanese technology burying a new generation of musicians and tech-savvy artists is pervasive. Our perception of the future began with this idea of ergonomic, click-switch functionality. Picking up from the sci-fi dreams of earlier cinema and television, music was the future's wet dream. But in truth, outside the wealthy players—ELP, Tangerine Dream, and similar 'progressives'—this more embryonic period was built upon a much more prosaic repurposing of our post-war tech world. It was, for youth like us, moneyless and involved simple electronics, home-built tools, primitive VCOs, filters, fuzz boxes made from Practical Electronics' circuit designs, decommissioned military tape recorders, and ad hoc tape delays.

The dream was not Korg or Yamaha, but the British-built EMS machines, which augmented their complex synthesisers with toylike touch-sensitive keys. Electronic music was emerging from lab coat experimentalism, and musique concrete, in our case, of Cabaret Voltaire, in a tiny loft in Sheffield, but touched by the glamorous, from-another-planet affectations of David Bowie and Eno's Roxy Music. The future of music was one of hot-styled 'make and make do', built from shortwave radio magazines, charity shop guitars, Woolworth's makeup counter, and army surplus chic.

The everyday DIY reality was not a barrier, merely an inconvenience, and on the whole, a creative prompt. As a generation born of TV and the beginnings of cheap travel, we were opened up to speculative worlds and exotic possibilities. We were overrun by imagination. In truth, the vacuum that money's absence afforded was filled up with exploration of the massive unknown; busy, enquiring, restless minds. We were youthful in a very evocative time and a very media-saturated space. The opportunities to dig and question were like air: We sucked it in, used it, and blew it out. Our access to everything in front of us was unique. McLuhan's communicated and connected global village enabled us. It offered autodidactic opportunities unavailable to previous generations; information at this moment, before it became monetised data, was plentiful, empowering, and motivating. What we didn't know didn't scare us, but it provoked us. Technology provided both agency and facility. It filled the sky with images and sounds we could play with, new worlds, like minds, speculative pathways out of a drab reality. It provided the means by which we could express their meaning for us, and it suggested how we could play them. It was all accessible; it was all culture; it was all popular. Pop was grain, texture, noise, and colour. Colour was pop.

As the decade rolled on, music became increasingly rendered by these shiny new machines. Synthesisers augmented guitars and drums. Joy Division, the perfect barometer, in their final moments, drifted into a rich new sound, paving the way for the New Order to follow. In the case of acts like the Human League, Gary Numan, and Depeche Mode, traditional instruments were replaced altogether, synthesisers creating familiar but ersatz, and novel, sounds. Others saw a different application of these technologies, their potential to divert the power latent within the system. As punk, at its most fundamental, had tapped into an important resistance, a need to challenge the accepted order, we and others saw the need to completely ditch the form and content to truly disrupt. We ourselves, but Throbbing Gristle in particular, felt it necessary to push the raw energy of the sounds, images, and words into new shapes rather than emulate pop and rock's conventional forms. It was simply not enough to apply faux instrument sounds in the belief you were creating something new; only real change could be achieved by subverting the technology. Discard, or hack the manual; a new counterculture that, by distorting any intended use, and simply overreaching, saw it was possible to transform things, to give us new eyes and ears.

Electricity comes from other planets, Lou Reed told us. We merged the power sounds of the city into the new electronic palette. To a constant backdrop of arc furnaces, incessant factory drones, interjected by the metallic pop and crash of steel, we imagined the noises of the new. Mutating industrial power into technologically rendered sounds, until now, unheard. Music from another planet. The key element that enabled this sonic alchemy was 'the studio.' Until this point, recording, as part of the making and selling operation, was in the grip of a corporate music industry: formalised, regulated, expensive, and largely divorced from the creative part of the process.

Emerging electronic music shattered this component of the industry cartel; it took ownership of how and where music could be made, feeding into a burgeoning, hungry, independent label culture. Rough Trade, Factory, Fast, Industrial, Mute, all began to break the corporate monopoly, all provided opportunities for the new artists to be heard. New voices, new sounds. The importance of this lies in how the studio, no longer just a means to capture performance as a 'record' to be marketed and sold, or an indulgent artist's playroom, rather became an instrument in its own right. Affordable, accessible, a space to play, a home of experimentation, and a tool of creation. For myself, as Cabaret Voltaire, this building of our own 'sound factory,' a kind of low-budget hybrid of Andy Warhol's loft space and Kraftwerk's Kling Klang, offered self-sufficiency and became intrinsic to the whole making and releasing of music, away from prying ears. For electronic and post-punk artists of the time, independence gave control, the ability to choose where, when, and how they functioned. This domestication of recording, helped by more new, readily available technology, preempted the growth of late-century musicmaking. The autonomy of the process began here; it was the twinkle in the eye of a million bedroom studios that today lie at the heart of contemporary music. Artists controlled the electricity.

Nothing is new; nothing is lost. We built on the old to create the new. The traditions of montage and 'objets trouvés,' Duchamp's 'ready mades,' provided an effective process of building the reality of the world around us into the work. Breaking our world apart and putting it back together in new shapes. The cutup techniques of William Burroughs and Brion Gysin, the collages John Heartfield and Kurt Schwitters, were applied to television samples, recording of political radio, underground film grabs, newspaper clippings, and images.

The medium varied, but the medium was, indeed, the message. Tools in the shape of tape recorders and Super-8 film allowed us to capture this newly saturated world, to bend and reshape it to our own style. The subsequent technologies of video recording and audio sampling would enable immediate, quick-fire responses—our Western Works studio had the TV set to record twenty-four hours a day, seven days a week. Old techniques, new applications.

For myself, the merging of the industrial sounds of the city and the future came increasingly through the vector of rhythm. The shape of the responses came from our long-standing connection to the beat. Seeped in soul, funk, and ska as young kids, we would push on with the Cabs during the eighties through our teenage affection to the sounds of the night. But it required technology to articulate this new rhythm age. Freed from the dependence upon cumbersome drum kits, and the chaos of rogue drummers, we now had drum machines, arpeggiators, and sequencers, our mechanisms of change. CV (control voltage)-gate, and MIDI (musical instrument digital interface) means by which these machines could connect to each other became more widely used, enabling them to tightly synchronise, to talk and dance with each other, driven by rhythm. The *New York Times* writer Jon Pareles made the point that it was the century of rhythm—the tempo of industry, the beat of technology, the pulse of the city. The repetition of rhythm, its hypnotic hold, all reinforced by the revived 12-inch format. The 12-inch became the default for club releases, extending the duration of tracks, opening them up to freestyle dubbed-out mixes. These were records that could push the low-end frequencies, through supercharged, often handcrafted sound systems. The politics of change was taking place in the darker subliminal spaces; the body became the locus, waiting for the soon-to-come ecstatic release.

Time is sequential, but fluid; we structure our own ideas in order to help us make sense of how things happen and why. Decades offer convenient points of transition, but in truth, things are much more complex and compound. This late-century period was without question a time of significant change, of uncertainty and premillennial shift and drift. Perhaps the real decade of sound happened in reaction to the periods in flux preceding them: 1976–1988. A less arbitrary, more considered epoch, in which popular culture, driven by technology, and generational, youthful, energy reshaped our lives in response. The upheavals of the early to mid-1970s, and the mid-1980s, both periods of conflict: war, strikes, and social unrest, which in turn saw riposte through the emergence of punk, post-punk, and the later explosive club cultures of house and techno. All spikes in the system. Electronic music, and the technologies it used, both catalysed and configured these changes. It is not a formula or a neat linear trajectory, but an acknowledgment of change, of action and reaction: a dialectic and a sonic synthesis. A volatile but notable and authentic period for music in which uncertainty, hope, and blind faith made everything alive and possible.

Stephen Mallinder
(Cabaret Voltaire)
2022

# INTRODUCTION

B ritain during the 1970s was a country and culture in flux, and the threat of nuclear war, mass unemployment, and strikes made it a particularly gloomy period. This was mediated through the media via disquieting TV theme music and supernatural shows, such as *Children of the Stones*. The modern world was on its way as giant concrete tower blocks paved the way toward a new decade. Further to this:

> There were few distractions; television closed down early, video was yet to arrive, computer games were crude, food was functional. LPs and singles were expensive and thus treasured, as were books. Britain has not yet made the shift from a largely literary culture to the overwhelmingly visual one of today (Lay 2007, 54).

The use of the synthesizer has spurred many fundamental shifts in the mechanisms of musicmaking and within this, a growing number of electronic acts were using the synthesizer to soundtrack-changing times. Along with the popularisation of the non-musician and the musical aesthetics established by both the Punk (ca. 1974–1980) and Post-Punk (ca. 1978–1984) movements, the synthesizer led to new and innovative effects, ideas, and processes. In parallel, some acts used such approaches in musicmaking in 1970s Britain to reflect the social and political climate at the time. Many of these acts would go on to influence the more commercial sound of synthesised popular music during the 1980s, which, in turn, shaped the sound of mainstream electronic music today.

*Dark Waves* examines the role of the synthesizer and electronics in shaping the dark and dystopian sound of electronic music in 1970s Britain, presenting a collected musicological analysis of the acts Cabaret Voltaire,

1

Throbbing Gristle, the Normal, Fad Gadget, the Human League, Gary Numan, and Visage, and it considers the background, influences, and technological approaches to each work. Further to this, an analysis of a seminal work of each act is presented, exploring and considering the production, track by track.

Part 1, 'Background Noise,' attempts to contextualise the social and cultural landscape of Britain in the mid- to late 1970s. Chapter 1, 'Dystopian Sentimentalities,' explores the idea of dystopianism and presents a number of early literary works within the field while at the same time considers both the cultural and technological factors that affected the development of the acts presented. Chapter 2, 'Political, Economic, and Social Influences,' is concerned with government structure and major policies during this period, detailing how major urban areas were going under a transformative change as tower blocks and urban areas were decentralising communities. This, coupled with oil shortages, strikes, and the threat of nuclear war saw Britain lose its grasp and direction, which, in turn, allowed for subcultural divisions such as Punk, to appear.

Chapter 3, 'Technology and Aesthetical Frameworks,' considers the popularisation of the synthesizer and uses a number of approaches, including technological determinism and cybernetics, in an attempt to address how technology influences both human action and thought. Many of these approaches are based on the historical observation that technologies are often released without thought given toward their impact. Further to this, it again examines the synthesizer in its development of new approaches and aesthetics. The synthesizer, which was once only in the hands of the few (primarily progressive rock bands) soon became available with the advent of Japanese synthesizers. Through this, musicians, and indeed non-musicians, could now generate the sounds of the future, broadly contextualising how musicians were using the synthesizer as a conduit for nonconformity and musical subversion.

Part 2, 'Outsider Electronics,' discusses how many of the acts documented in this publication were influenced by seminal art movements, and in this, would go on to inform their aesthetics and sound. Chapter 4, 'Cabaret Voltaire: Dadaism Up North,' examines the seminal act whose work consisted primarily through the experimentation with DIY electronics and tape machines, as well as Dada-influenced performances. Finding an audience during the Post-Punk era, Cabaret Voltaire integrated their experimental sensibilities and were the most innovative and influential electronic groups of their era. This chapter focuses on the band's approach and the impact of their album *Mix Up* (1979).

Chapter 5, 'Throbbing Gristle: Music from the Death Factory,' examines the acts' evolution from the experimental performance art group COUM Transmissions to a musical act. This chapter examines the band's diverse range of influences: transgressive and confrontational aesthetics as well as sound manipulation (noise; pre-recorded tape-based samples), influenced by the work of William S. Burroughs and Brion Gysin. Their seminal album, *20 Jazz Funk Greats* (1979), is presented for discussion.

Science fiction and electronic music have always shared thematic ideals, and Chapter 6, 'The Normal: The Car Crash Set,' documents Daniel Miller's *The Normal,* an act majorly influenced by the works of J.G. Ballard, in particular *Crash* (1973). The release of *T.V.O.D./Warm Leatherette* in 1978 and the Mute Records in 1979, a label that would go on to shape the electronic sound of the 1980s and beyond, positioned Miller as a key figure of influence.

A number of the acts included for discussion would not go on to gain the same levels of respect and recognition for their music, as Chapter 7, 'Fad Gadget: Mechanised Curiosity,' documents. The work and life of Frank Tovey (1956–2002) and Fad Gadget represent an act that would change and morph (musically) with the times. Although his early work was largely ignored at the time, Tovey's contribution would go on to inform the sound of Post-Punk and industrial music in both Europe and the United States, through his album *Fireside Favourites* (1980).

Part 3, 'Crossing the Mainstream,' examines acts that crossed over into the popular consciousness and zeitgeist. Chapter 8, 'The Human League: Electronically Yours,' documents the act's earlier days, when they were an experimental act, until a split saw members go their separate ways, resulting in Heaven 17 and a much more commercially orientated Human League Mark II. Technologically, the act was ground-breaking, and this is discussed via their album *Reproduction* (1979).

During 1977–1980, some artists were accused of being pastiche, and their music and contributions became mocked (particularly by the press). Chapter 9, 'Gary Numan: Subhuman in Suburbia,' documents Numan's rise to fame and his not-only-mainstream appeal but his commercial crossover. His work, particularly with the Mini-Moog synthesizer, would feature heavily in the work that is reviewed, *The Pleasure Principle* (1979).

As the synthesised musical landscape became more and more commercialised, the dominance of fashion and style would play a major factor in the success for many acts of the 1980s. Chapter 10, 'Visage: The New Guard,' documents the group and is discussed in relation to its collaborative effect. Essentially a studio group, the New Guard was fronted by Steve Strange and musically directed by Midge Ure, who would go on to have even more success fronting Ultravox. Their album *Visage* (1980) is presented here as a document for changing times, breaking the dystopian for something to help with an optimistic viewpoint at the cusp of a new decade.

Chapter 11, 'Conclusion: Influence and Afterword,' analyses how these acts worked against the backdrop of the feelings of social alienation that many of the movement's key participants and fans were experiencing at the time. These acts were making music during the Punk movement, and while they were both concerned with rewriting musical norms, they, in many ways, created an alternative world viewpoint, one that dealt with themes of isolation and despair, mediated with sounds that seemed to have come from another planet. The chapter also examines the influence of the acts discussed, highlighting how dystopian pop crept (subconsciously and consciously) into the mainstream and the UK Charts via acts like Depeche Mode and Duran Duran during the mid- to late 1980s.

The legacy of the acts presented in the book is evident across all forms of popular electronic musicmaking today. However, academically, as no such collection exists, *Dark Waves* aims to shed further light on this monumental and influential movement and moment of both technological and cultural significance.

# I

## BACKGROUND NOISE

# 1

## DYSTOPIAN SENTIMENTALITIES

D ystopia is the creation of other worlds, imagined far in the future, and it can be defined by an array of terms, primarily related to societal issues, including notions of repression of independent thought maintained by government, corporate, bureaucratic, or technological control. Within this was the controller and the protagonist; the former is responsible for the surveillance and uniformity of the latter. With such levels of oppression, questions of oppression and untrust give way to the formation of its associated mindset. Before dystopia, utopia, or an ideal set of conditions, often set with impossible ideals. Often it was in this mindset of writers that such worlds were born. Indeed, its Greek translation suitably places it as οὐ ('not') and τόπος ('place'). This chapter examines the above while considering topics such as 'psychogeography' and cultural issues.

The onset of the global COVID pandemic has seen a rise in popularity of dystopian fiction, and indeed, television, with series like Charlie Brooker's *Black Mirror*, *The Hunger Games*, and the adaptation of Margaret Atwood's *The Handmaid's Tale* captivating us with extreme levels of pessimism. While these shows may relate to our lived experiences in some light, they no doubt raise levels of both cultural and social anxiety and of the notion of how people with power can manipulate the population through fear, oppression, and impoverishment, is critical in understanding the concept of the 'dystopian machine.'

Dystopian sentimentalities first appeared within key works of fiction, including *Mundus Alter ET Idem (The World Different and the Same)* by Joseph Hall, first published in 1596. It paints a roundly negative critique of society at the time. It documents a messenger, Mercurius Brittanicus, on a voyage to Terra Australis Incognita (now Antarctica). On his arrival, Mercurius discovers a world where the norms of society are exaggerated, ultimately revealing its faults. Mercurius questions man's weakness and his appetite for vices. A deep feeling of cynicism fills his soul on departure from this new world.

The book points its finger toward the ambitious and the free-spirited, and its publication is said to have heavily influenced Jonathan Swift's *Gulliver's Travels*, published in 1726. H.G. Wells ended the Victorian era with the publication in 1899 of *When the Sleeper Awakes*, revised and republished in 1910 as *The Sleeper Awakes*. The story, in which a dream becomes reality, sees the protagonist awake in 2100 to a world ruthlessly governed by a harsh dictatorship. Two key dystopian themes are born within *When the Sleeper Awakes*—the use of technology as a tool of manipulation and the advent of the subterranean. More importantly, the book helped set a thematic path toward a number of seminal British works that explore with the dystopian mindset: *Nineteen Eighty-Four* by George Orwell and *Brave New World* by Aldous Huxley.

The role of society and technology is beautifully played out in E.M. Forster's short story *The Machine Stops*, first published in 1909. The story tells of a population that lives in small pods buried within vast catacombs underneath sprawling cities. All is controlled and provided for by 'The Machine,' including the provision of food, shelter, and more importantly, communication. In this world, technology provides and submits to your every need:

> Then she generated the light, and the sight of her room, flooded with radiance and studded with electric buttons, revived her. There were buttons and switches everywhere—buttons to call for food for music, for clothing. There was the hot-bath button, by pressure of which a basin of (imitation) marble rose out of the floor, filled to the brim with a warm deodorised liquid. There was the cold-bath button. There was the button that produced literature. And there were of course the buttons by which she communicated with her friends. The room, though it contained nothing, was in touch with all that she cared for in the world. (Forster 1909, 130)

Forster predicted that technology would  become central to the human condition. He pointed out that our race needed it for survival, while at the same time, he cautioned on its overreliance. These publications provide a basis and insight into the misuse of power and technology, and the implications of technology are clear, and indeed, more vivid today than ever before, through the use and misuse of technology.

What seems more pertinent to this discussion is the 'dystopian sentimentalities' question as both in fiction, and as we shall document, in electronic musicmaking in Britain during 1973–1983, it was perhaps a sense of loss of individualism and alienation that became its driving force. Such undercurrents were supported further by the rise of a computerised society where many were rebelling against both streamlining and at the same time, corrosion of conformity.

During the period of 1973–1983, technology was developing autonomously; both society and its cultural outlets (music, film) were embracing its progression and its efficiency. Often, little regard is given toward the social and political implications that technology can generate. This diffusion of technology has infiltrated commerce, education, government, and popular music, through the use of the synthesizer, as it has now become a conduit for musicians acting as a vehicle for innovation in sound, a sound that can extend and break from the traditional parameters of popular music, used as a conduit to provoke the generation of 'imagined places,' and for some, a dystopian sound: oppressive, controlling, and dehumanised.

## ARBITRARY ROUTES

In order to further define the creation of this so-called dystopian sound, an important part of the relationship between the acts reviewed in this book is that of place and its geographical effect on their resulting outputs. Within this, we have to consider what it means to the effects of location on the development of a 'dystopian sound,' and the concept of psychogeography allows us to fully explore and discuss this. The history and evolution of the term can be traced to three thinkers—Charles Baudelaire, Walter Benjamin, and Guy Debord—and much of these observations are seen through the viewpoint of the 'flâneur': 'a figure of the modern artist-poet, a figure keenly aware of the bustle of modern life, an amateur detective and investigator of the city, but also a sign of the alienation of the city and of capitalism' (Shaya 2004, 22).

With the onset of modernism and the Industrial Revolution, Baudelaire painted a distinct sense of the modern cityscape and the urban experience. Images of this meta-being appear in a poem like 'Le Soleil' from the *Tableaux Parisiens* section of the second edition of *Les Fleurs du Mal* (1861), in the 'duelling in dark corners for a rhyme / and stumbling over words like cobblestones.'[1] Baudelaire was exploring Paris as a dark and hostile environment under the influence of various opioids, so his writings were tinged with surrealism and depth.

The flâneur was the birth of the outsider, and as we know, the realm of the outsider has always been at the heart of esoteric and experimental electronic and industrial music. Such themes appear across his work, most notably in his work *The Painter of Modern Life* (1863). Here Baudelaire saw modernity as evolutionary, ever changing in that 'modernity is the transitory, the fleeting [le fugitif], the contingent, half of art [la moitié de l'art], the other half of which is the eternal and the unchangeable' (Baudelaire 1863, IV 553). The beauty within the urban was fleeting, and indeed it transformed ideas of beauty, as 'at a stroke, or a couple of strokes, Baudelaire transforms, or claims to, both the likely subject matter and the evaluation criteria for art. The whole hold of contemporary life and manners is opened up as worth representing, worth making into art— as having its own beauty' (Bowlby 2004, 47). Baudelaire would go on to directly influence classifications of art analysis and criticism.

His work would massively influence Walter Benjamin (1892–1940) and his *The Arcades Project* (1924–1940), in which he reevaluated art versus the modern world and art versus nature. The life of philosopher and culture critic Benjamin was complex. He died at the age of forty-eight while fleeing from the Nazis in Portbou, Spain; at the time, he was in the middle of completing the manuscript. *The Arcades Project* subject is that of the consumer arades of Paris and the significance of what they symbolise, both past and the future, and he saw these as markers of changing social ideals; buying items was just as addictive as opium, and he viewed consumerism as a distraction (and a threat) to nature. However, Benjamin took influence from Baudelaire and brought the flâneur (albeit now more of an idle, coffee-drinking people-watcher) back into the urban sphere and consciousness.

Finally published in 1982, the work itself, said to be tedious and unhumorous, remains linked in the evolution of the commodification of things—and his speculative discourse on this paved the way for the next wave of theorists within the evolution of the idea and influence of place.

Paris again was the scene of the next wave of urban explorists, and during the mid-1950s, the term *psychogeography* was coined by the Marxist theorist and Letterist Internationalist[2] founder Guy Debord. Taking from both Baudelaire and Benjamin, this form, what is referred to as 'cognitive geography,' relied on more of a personal and emotional connection to the urban landscape with Debord describing it as:

The practice of defamiliarization and the choice of encounters, the sense of incompleteness and ephemerality, the love of speed transposed onto the plane of the mind, together with inventiveness and forgetting are among the elements of an ethics of drifting we have already begun to test in the poverty of the cities of our time (Debord cited in Bishop ed. 2006, 23).

An environment could both alter mood and influence behaviour. It's obvious, even from the outset of this book, that the cities in which they produced their seminal works had a monumental influence on their sonic worlds(s), perhaps more so for acts like Cabaret Voltaire, in which Sheffield, psychogeographically, played a role in their musical output and perspectives; such will be documented in each chapter.

## CULTURAL LAGS

The American sociologist William F. Ogburn coined the term *cultural lag theory* in his work *Social Change with Respect to Culture and Original Nature* (1922), suggesting that technology was the primary engine of progress, but tempered by social responses to it. He defined the way in which culture often takes time to catch up with its own innovations and that this (lag) creates both social conflicts and dynamanisms:

The thesis is that the various parts of modern culture are not changing at the same rate, some parts are changing more rapidly than others; and that since there is a correlation and interdependence of parts, a radical change in one part of our culture requires readjustment through other changes in the various correlated parts of culture. (Ogburn 1922, 200–201)

This theory has been used (and somewhat) abused as it has often been implemented to address social problems. Ogburn saw the evolution of the lag theory via four operations and concepts: 'invention, accumulation, diffusion and adjustment' (Ibid., 75). Invention proposes toward the onset of new technologies and were viewed as collective contributions to society. When old inventions become obsolete, technology grows, and accumulation and a process of stockpiling occurs. Diffusion sees the spreading of an idea from one cultural group to another, which, in turn, combines with old inventions to bring about new ones. This is very much in line with the evolution of the synthesizer, particularly during the mid-1980s with the advent of MIDI. As a culture, we respond to invention and adjustment, and any delay in this can and will essentially cause a (cultural) lag.

Culture for Ogburn was, in many ways, a microcosm, and his followup, *On Culture and Change* (1964), examined the social trends as technology's influence became more and more dominant throughout the 1960s, examining technology, governmental change, and how inventions altered the standard of living. One key element in his work, as discussed briefly above, is that of diffusion, and within this, for each new invention, some major or minor social change and adjustment must be made. He defined this as as a 'combination of existing and known elements of culture, material and/or nonmaterial, or a modification of one to form a new one' (Ibid., 23). What is really pertinent to his theories is the use of technological means to examine culture and social change from a sociological perspective, an area that resonates within this book.

In the case of the synthesizer, technological means altered the paradigm of traditional musicmaking and its resulting sound. It's not necessarily about where an invention is made or manufactured (Moog in the United States and EMS in the UK), culture may be influenced as a byproduct in any case. Further to this, with the advent of more affordable synthesizers, via both Korg and Roland during the period of 1977–1980, more and more people were playing synthesised music, thus creating and/or contributing to social trends that reflected cultural shifts.

Further to this, geography comes into play: as London was the base for a number of the acts documented here, acts like Cabaret Voltaire were more culturally distanced from cities like London. However, as we shall see, distancing themselves from the influence of a major city allowed the group to completely reinvent themselves and thus became a truly unique 'invention' of their own. Thus, acts such as Cabaret Voltaire grew and propelled culture 'due to two features of the cultural process, one is the persistence of culture forms (tradition) and the other is the addition of new forms (invention)' (Ogburn 1947, 74).

## NOTES

1. Extracted from Charles Baudelaire, *The Sun, Les Fleurs du Mal*, trans. Richard Howard (London: Picador, 1987), 88.

2. Created by Guy Debord, Letterist Internationalist was a Paris-based collective of radical artists and theorists, and many of the group would go on to form the Situationist International (1957–1972).

# 2

# POLITICAL, ECONOMIC, AND
# CULTURAL INFLUENCES

In order to get a viewpoint of the contemporary vision of Britain in the 1970s, it is important to understand that the nation was undergoing a number of concurrent crises. Two political agendas shook the landscape during this period: the Industrial Relations Act (1971) and the Alternative Economic Strategy (AES). This chapter focuses on the knockoff effect from these policies. While political and economic crises have been the subject of numerous publications, both past and present, the analysis of these is kept to a brief overview. It also presents a number of cultural events that further shaped the landscape.

Political crises during this period were the result of the failures of post-war settlement, which were 'laid out to which a new order emerged itself potentially embodies an important (but often unacknowledged) set of politi-cised assumptions' (Black & Pemberton 2013, 2). Britain's entry into the EEC (European Economic Community) in 1973 could be seen as a symbol of a reconceptualization of the commonwealth, or indeed, the beginning of its decline in front of the eyes of the world, as common marketplace ideals were in direct opposition to the ongoing oil crisis, power cuts, and miner strikes ongoing at the time. The period of 1975 to 1979 polarised the conservative government, a period in which unemployment doubled. The inheritance from previous governments gave rise to 'legacy' issues, particularly in regard to inflation. The creeping inflation of the 1950s had long since developed an acceleration of its own, with successive reflationary bouts of public spending aimed at reducing unemployment.

Savings were destroyed scarcely before they had begun to grow, and inflation reached 30 percent in 1975, 'eroding international competitive-ness, creating long-term instability, obliterating profits, and engendering uncertainties for investment and ultimately jeopardising jobs' (Holmes

1985, 14). One major factor that spurred the government was the high taxation of the rich. This was offset by another inheritance from previous governments, unemployment. In some ways, unemployment in Britain during the late 1970s was a casualty of inflation, and the very nature of technological onset in society influenced the demand on labour and capital.

## (DE)POLITICISATION

Edward Heath's government hastily pushed through the Industrial Relations Act (1971), which sought to reform the unions. Labour failed to push through a similar plan in 1969, and insuch, the act set off clusters of industrial action across the nation. It has been suggested that the political impact of unions was widely perceived to have brought down governments in 1974 and 1979. Little political credit was given for the 'sacrifices made by union members, particularly in the public sector to see off hyper-inflation via the acceptance of reductions in real wages' (Black, Pemberton & Thane (eds). 2016, 8). The act also triggered strikes and prohibited limitations on legitimate strikes, and it would ultimately be the downfall of Heath's government. The climate of unfair industrial practices led to a wave of grassroot labour movements being created. Its background lies in the wildcat strikes of the 1960s, in which it was believed that the trade unions had lost control and a form of militant rank-and-file held their employers for ransom.[1]

The act would ultimately fail due to the government's interventionist[2] role within the trade unions. Nongovernmental forms of political action among rank-and-file trade unionists ensured the political space for deliberation around industrial relations reform remained wide open. The Industry Act (1975), passed by Harold Wilson's Labour government, followed. With a drive for increasing corporatism, the government was developing a new form of interventionism, in which the role of the state was to harness capitalism to the interests of all, and the role of business was to make a profit for Britain. The state now leaned toward an economy in which it could direct and control private business, a leaning that favours collectivism over individualism. The act was very much for the nation, not for class nor race, in that:

> The Industry Act therefore expresses the basic character of corporatism—an economic system which combines private ownership and State control. It contrasts with capitalism's private ownership and private control and with state socialism's, state ownership and State control. The Act also illustrates a fundamental principle of corporatist administration: the

avoidance of explicit legal codification of its control mechanisms. Of course, the emasculated piece of legislation that finally emerged does not establish corporatism in Britain but it should not be underestimated. It served to bring out into the open the principles of the economic system toward which Britain has been evolving over the past 15 years. It created two corporatist institutions which may become more powerful in future. It indicated the likely course of Britain's medium-term economic development, unless there is a significant shift in political power. That is its historical significance. (Phal & Winkler 1975, 106)

Much like the Industrial Relations Act, the act divided the nation (economically) as it focused on an aggressive protectionism of the nation's economic interests, suspicious of foreign companies and their agendas. The resistance, at the societal level, was a necessary part of understanding how the (de)politicised governance is shaped, imposed, transformed, and potentially undermined. Radical thinking was needed and came in the form of the Alternative Economic Strategy (AES). Dominating much of Labour's official programme during the periods of 1974 and 1979, and proposed by Tony Benn in 1976, it was a strategy in which:

> The government of national unity, the tory strategy of a pay policy, higher taxes all round and deflation, with Britain staying in the common market. Then Strategy B which is the real Labour policy of saving jobs, a vigorous micro-investment programme, import control, control of the banks and insurance companies, control of export, of capital, higher taxation of the rich, and Britain leaving the common market. (Benn 1989, 203)

Key to AES was the rapid recovery and modernisation of industry and addressing the ongoing recession. One of its more ambitious strands was to bring about the 'fundamental and irreversible shift of the balance of power and wealth in favour of working people and their families' (Rowthorn 1980, 85–94). Price controls on goods and compulsory planning on agreements would attempt to force big firms (especially multi-nationals) to pursue different production, employment, and investment strategies. Additionally, the public ownership of financial institutions was muted, which would allow more public control over investment portfolios in relation to pension funds.

Sadly, its most ambitious (and totally unachievable) aim was the redistribution of income and wealth with aim of eliminating gross societal inequalities, an objective naïve in nature and ill conceived in its proposition as 'its primary frame of reference is the nation, and many of its measures involve a unilateral attempt to weaken our links with the rest of the capitalist world, with the aim of strengthening Britain's power to make independent decisions. The strategy discounts the idea of a radical shift to the left in continental Europe in the near future, and its ideas on new forms of international cooperation are almost non-existent' (Rowthorn 1981, 5). The national dimensions of AES are clear, but it very much neglects an international dimension and perhaps, lacks vision. Such high ambitions were, no doubt, bound to fail, and ultimately the cabinet rejected Benn's AES in favour of a much more favourable loan from the International Monetary Fund on December 1, 1976.[3]

## HOME ECONOMICS

A concept referred to as Keynesian Economics are various macroeconomic theories about how economic output is strongly influenced by aggregate demand. In this Keynesian view, aggregate demand does not necessarily equal the productive capacity of the economy. Instead, it is influenced by a host of factors, ones considered in this chapter.

Britain's economy during the period of 1973–1983 could in many ways be viewed as a series of traumas: strikes and oil crises, to name a few. From OECD[4] reports, it seems that the 1950s and 1960s were the golden age of economic performance. Margaret Thatcher's conservative government began on May 4, 1979.

The ideological conflict between both Thatcher and Heath was evident and determined not to repeat both the Heath and Callaghan's governments. Thatcher focused on trying to halt Britain's economic decline and began to pick up the pieces left by legacy issues. What's interesting is that Thatcher's 'politics of decline,' an ethos that mirrors social and moral unrest, was an approach in which she based her claim to power on having the unique ability to reverse the country's decline.[5] Central to this narrative was the argument that the problems of the mid-1970s were not short term, but the 'culmination of a long-term decline, deeply embedded in British society and in its political economy' (Tomlinson in Black, Pemberton & Thane [eds.] 2013, 51).

## MORAL PANIC

The story of Britain in the 1970s is one of the attempted rise and management of a condition of rising inflation and rising unemployment and the exhaustion, first, of the Conservatives' and then of Labour's capacity to use incomes policies to manage inflationary pressures.[6] The Winter of Discontent (1978–1979) would prove, morally, to be bleak, and up to that point, unchartered waters for Britain. The roots of the dispute lie in the income policy of the 1970–1974 Conservative government of Heath, the 1973 oil crisis, and strikes in the mining industry that resulted in the 'Three Day Week' in early 1974. The radical left wing politics, leftover from the movements of the late 1960s, would go on to inform a new generation of thinkers and intellectuals who would use these crises discussed to inform the politics they would create.

This was a time for change, of considerable economic and political uncertainty, and as Stewart Holland's *The Socialist Challenge* (1975) outlined, it was an 'ambitious interventionist industrial strategy based around far-reaching measures of public ownership and planning' (Wicham-Jones 2013, 124).

## CONCLUSION

This period has had an enduringly negative image due to the economic and negative conditions that made it so. It is surprising, given both the many policy and institutional failures, the vast majority of the population continued to maintain their faith within its institutions. From the golden ages of the 1950–1960s, the 1970s was the decline of the empire, yet it also signalled a time of great social change. Women's liberation came (via its inroads made in the United States), allowing identity and awareness of issues like equal pay to become more important in public consciousness, and further to this, the rise of feminism underpinned a significant role in how activism could (and did) play within social change. Within the more established realms of intellectualism, the university sector (particularly some of its younger employees) grew tired of the old system, damning the old rule of law, and their attitudes and viewpoints would have caused a trickle-down effect to students who were of a similar frame of mind, bemused by the socio-political environment at the time.

The Punk movement was seminal in playing a pivotal role, and for many in the adaptation of its ethos, it became a lifestyle choice for many youths in Britain. In 1976 and having just signed to EMI records, the Sex

Pistols' *Anarchy in the UK* was unleashed on the public on November 26, positioning Punk in a newly politicised attitude. Its opening line was part mantra, part threat to the empire and old guard, with Lydon spitting, 'I am an antichrist' in the song's opening lines. It was nihilistic and raw, a callout to the youth and an ideology for change in music, an opportunity to mix things up.

One event on Thames Television in December 1976 exposed the nation to the dangers of the movement, to the so-called sick and sinister movements. Beamed into homes of millions of British bystanders, a promo for the single, an interview on Granada Television with Bill Grundy (at barely 90 seconds), would demonstrate their antiestablishment and disruptive best, when guitarist Steve Jones referring to Grundy as a 'dirty old man.'[7] Jones, on national television, was announcing his challenge to the old guard and bluntly commenting on how youth culture felt about the system. Stanley Cohen's *Folk Devils and Moral Panics* (1972) suggests that moral judgments are 'constructed,' in that:

> The problem is the nature of the condition—'what actually happened. Questions of symbolism, emotion and representation cannot be translated into comparable sets of statistics. Qualitative terms like 'appropriateness' convert the nuances of moral judgement more accurately than the (implied) quantitative measure of 'disproportionate'—but the more they do so, the more obviously they are socially constructed. (Cohen 1972, 29)

Cohen questions societal response and whether it was appropriate or if mass media were the moral judges. The aftermath of the appearance, this display of anti-ethos, blatant respect for the elders on live TV, saw the traditional media and musicmaking mechanisms immediately cutting ties with such viewpoints: tabloids were the first to respond with memorable headlines like 'The Filth and the Fury'[8] and 'The Punk Rock Horror Show.' The BBC were soon to follow, blacklisting the single, while EMI dropped the act, showcasing that the establishment would simply not tolerate such damming outbursts at the centre stage of society.

It also highlights that what they achieved and did was certainly not an isolated incident, but it was and would become part of a wider, more integrated social perspective. Ultimately, the nation's reaction to the Sex Pistols' appearance on Granada Television created a moral panic, which had its own trajectory, or 'a microphysics of outrage—which however, is initiated and sustained by wider social and political forces' (Ibid., 31). As this book attempts to document, many of the acts lived through these 'moral panics,' and some attempted to channel this into their work, which in turn produced some of their most influential works. Ultimately, they used technology to channel the hopeless and dystopian dreams the nation had.

## NOTES

1. Many thought the trade union 'problem' would have to be solved, as wage drift inflation soon outstripped improvements in productivity.

2. As suggested by Sam Warner in https://blogs.lse.ac.uk/politicsandpolicy/why-did-the-industrial-relations-act-1971-fail-depoliticisation-and-the-importance-of-resistance/ (accessed March 22, 2022).

3. See Benn (1989, 31).

4. OECD: Organisation for Economic Cooperation and Development.

5. See Lawrence Black, Hugh Pemberton, Pat Thane (2013, 44).

6. Ibid., 58.

7. See Savage (1991, 257–59).

8. *Daily Mirror*, December 2, 1976.

# 3

# TECHNOLOGY AND AESTHETICAL FRAMEWORKS

The synthesizer represents one of the most significant cultural developments of twentieth-century popular musicmaking, and one consequence of an increasingly technologized culture is the oversight of what machines like these had, all before the dominance of digital signal processing. This chapter examines the rise of the synthesizer in popular music in Britain by considering the seminal events, in both the United States and then the UK, and the technological shift that it brought about. It also presents two aesthetical frameworks—technological determinism and cybernetics—in an attempt to discuss approaches brought about via the synthesizer. Finally, it considers a faithful June 1972 broadcast of Roxy Music's appearance on BBC's Old Grey Whistle Test, when Brian Eno presented his EMS VCS3 synthesizer to millions of viewers, changing the direction of countless musicians, helping them to reconsider the traditional instruments upon which they had been relying.

## THE SYNTHESIZER: ACROSS THE POND

Within popular music history, we can trace the synthesizer's introduction through a number of well-known productions, primarily in the United States. The United States of America (1967–1968), and their use of the synthesizer, had quite an influence on the counterculture music of the late 1960s in the United States.

Unusually, the band had no guitar player; instead, they used strings, keyboards, and electronics, including primitive synthesizers and various audio processors. They presented a more radical sense of politics, aesthetics, and religious/philosophical aspects of 1960s counterculture, a dark contrast to the oncoming philosophy of free love and peace. The band's leader, Joseph Byrd, a Los Angeles–based composer, helped bring early synthesizers, the avant-garde, and classical aesthetics to popular musicmaking, establishing a role that synthesizers could potentially possess: that of radical and cultural subversion, through sound.

*Switched-On Bach* (1968), by Wendy Carlos, represented a true turning point for the synthesizer. Not only was it a commercial success, it also contributed to the machine's growing interest within the general public. The limitations of the early Moog synthesizer used on *Switched-On Bach* are often overlooked, as the instrument was monophonic. Bob Moog built a component especially for Carlos that triggered chords, and upon advice from Carlos, key sensitivity was introduced to the instrument, but unlike a conventional piano, there were no sustain or expression pedals. The different voices and elements had to be painstakingly tracked and layered in the studio: Expressions were added by adjusting filters, while oscillator and envelope controls were played with one hand while melodies were played with the other.

Rather viewing the synthesizer as a quirky new toy, the album ultimately helped showcase it and its apparent limitless sound-generation possibilities. *Switched-On Bach* went on to be the first classical album to go platinum in America, remaining at number one on the classical-album charts for more than three years, peaking at number ten on the pop charts of 1972.

The 1970s was a hedonistic time for musicians who used synthesizers, and from this, two distinct classes of users were born: explorers and virtuosos. Bands like Tangerine Dream utilised the synthesizer to slip into the unconscious, to charter far-out worlds, while the latter included groups like Emmerson, Lake, and Palmer, who were using the synthesizer to demonstrate musical skills, lost behind walls of electronic devices. Their sound was often shaped by variations on classical music's old reliables: fugues and arpeggios, as heard in Emerson Lake and Palmer's 1977 LP, *Fanfare for the Common Man*, adapted from Aaron Copland's 1942 piece of the same name. Thus, each class of player helped shape the sound of the synthesizer in the 1970s on a more commercially driven level.

Simon Reynolds's *Guardian* article, 'One Nation under a Moog,' points toward two additional phases the synthesizer went through during the 1980s, the first of which relied on science fiction–based concepts like dystopia and dehumanisation, as it attempted to reflect the social and political climate at the time with acts like Gary Numan being core to this movement. The second phase was far more commercially successful as a reaction against the use of the synthesizer to portray a darker side of electronic music music-making, as seen by acts like Soft Cell, which helped shape the sound of 1980s synth pop, which, in turn, helped shape the sound of current mainstream electronic music. Reynolds observed that:

> Electronic sounds now suggested jaunty optimism and the gregariousness of the dancefloor, they evoked a bright, clean future just round the corner rather than JG Ballard's desolate 70s cityscapes. And the subject matter for songs mostly reverted to traditional pop territory: love and romance, escapism and aspiration. (Reynolds, 2009)

Reynolds further alludes to this second wave's more valuable contribution: that of the synthesizer having the power to harness, again quite successfully on a commercial level, electronic music with soul. This came to the forefront in the mid-1980s with acts like Yazoo and Erasure fully embracing the synthesizer's potential for this aspect. For the purpose of this book, the discussion points toward the first wave in the use of the synthesizer.

The synthesizer helped spur toward a number of fundamental shifts within the mechanisms of popular musicmaking. Methodologies within the synthesizer's instrument design and architecture, one that stretches back fifty years, exploit traditional signal processing applications. As an instrument, its design history, within popular music, can be traced back to the early 1960s in the United States, when East Coast (Bob Moog) and West Coast (Don Buchla) manufacturers began with a modular approach to sound synthesis. Due to the demand for more portable and affordable options, Moog, in particular, turned to more fixed architecture and consumer-based approaches. During the late 1960s, people were obliged to perceive the synthesizer in terms of instruments with which they were familiar, such as the piano or the guitar, and escaping from these shadows proved to be difficult at first. Mark Brend points toward this in 'The Sound of Tomorrow: How Electronic Music Was Smuggled into the Mainstream,' in that:

> (Electronic music) is not a cautious departure from certain traditional paths but rather, in the radical character of its techniques, gives us access to sound phenomena hitherto unknown in the field of music. This bursting open of our familiar world of sound by electronic means leads to new musical possibilities of a wholly unpredictable nature. (Brend 2012, 33)

This 'unpredictable nature' was often explored by the non-musician. Aided by the prompt of the Punk movement and its aesthetics, the form of musician, with no formal musical training, could easily create real-time responses to sound, producing more flexible, tangible, and versatile musical experiences. Through this, part of the reward in using the synthesizer is that users learn about their operation of the synthesizer during the musicmaking process, and for the non-musician, making music with a synthesizer is, for the most part, a process of exploration that often produces unexpected results and sounds.

## THE SYNTHESIZER: TECHNOLOGY AND GESTURE

The functional limitations of early synthesizers, ones used by the acts documented in this book, influenced the resultant sounds they produced. This, it is suggested, allows users of the synthesizer to become closer to the electronic behaviour of sound generation during its creation rather than something that is preplanned, with sheet music being a prime example here. One key element to the synthesizer, in particular an analogue one, is its control interface and its tactile approach to musicmaking. This hands-on approach influences the types of sounds and gestures that can be obtained from it. The multifunctionality of digital synthesizers[1] can present a hindrance of sorts within the compositional process as it possesses infinite possibilities and sound-making options. The control of sound with just one knob brings about one of the (analogue) synthesiser's major contributions, that of the limited control of expressiveness and gesture—elements sometimes lost in translation within the use of digital synthesizers.

Electronic musicmaking began in the radio studios of Europe during the 1950s, most notably at WDR (Westdeutscher Rundfunk) in Cologne and Radio France in Paris, when what was referred to as 'specialised equipment' was repurposed as 'instruments' as composers such as Karlheinz Stockhausen and Piere Boulez began to use them both for sound generation and for manipulation. Soon they would be at the forefront at the borders of sound exploration, born without reference to musical tradition.

David Keane, in his essay, 'At the Threshold of an Aesthetic,' referred to the work of such composers as working 'without reference to human gesture' (Keane 1981, 99). This tradition continued throughout the 1950s and early 1960s. It would be the introduction of voltage-controlled synthesizers at the end of the 1960s that would push the sound of the synthesizer closer to the edge of popular music fields. As the budgets for electronic music studios grew smaller and smaller, composers began to migrate from hardware to computer-aided composition in the quest for the new.

Musical performance, in a cultural context, has always been inextricably linked with the body, and its physicality is evident. Further to this, the tactile nature of the synthesizer allows it to be more gestural than traditional instruments, thus providing a heightened sense of interaction for its users. Music technology changed dramatically during the 1970s, and while musical aesthetics requires reflection and development benefiting from longer historical periods, electronic music production is now largely supported by a diverse industrial base devoted to its marketing and development. In this situation, an awareness of an instrument's physicality can influence some musical instrument design approaches.

## AESTHETICAL FRAMEWORKS: TECHNOLOGICAL DETERMINISM AND AGENCY

In order to discuss, aesthetically, the use of the synthesizer, the first theoretical framework examined is the area of technological determinism (TD). Technology develops autonomously; we embrace its progression as it propels our culture at breakneck speed, toward a future that is hard to see clearly. The synthesizer, as a conduit for creation, has facilitated the musician or producer to take a more functional role by simply becoming a controller, thus allowing the synthesizer to become the primary compositional element.

Is the synthesizer independent of external influence, or is it solely determined by the human will of the player? One approach, technological determinism, attempts to address such a question as it seeks to understand how technology influences human action and thought. Much of its approach is based on the historical observation that technologies are often released without thought given toward their impact, and while some technologies may transform societies and cultures in significant ways, others may not. Along with TD, the concept of agency should be considered. Agency is an intersection of power, from where power is distributed into the different hands and directions, and in this case, the synthesizer.

In 'On Technological Determinism: A Typology, Scope Conditions and a Mechanism,' Dafoe (2015) elaborates on agency:

> A central issue in the study of technology is the question of agency. To what extent do we have control over the tools we use—and hence also our systems of production, social relations, and worldview. To what extent are our technologies thrust upon us—by controlling elites, by

path-dependent decisions from the past, or by some internal technological logic? (Dafoe 2015, 1048)

Through this, agency entails the claim that musicians *do*, in fact, make
decisions, as Mayr (2011) in *Authority, Liberty, & Automatic Machinery in
Early Modern Europe* points out, in that:

> Our self understanding as human agents includes commitment to three
> crucial claims about human agency: That agents must be active, that
> actions are part of the natural order, and that intentional actions can be
> explained by the agent's reasons for acting. (Mayr 2011, I)

Through the very act of performing or recording with a synthesizer, such
observations point out that while these elements are indispensable, they are
in conflict and tension with one another. How much does the synthesizer
engage with the capacity of individuals to act independently and to make
their own free choices?

A number of factors should be considered here: (a) the relationship
between the synthesizer and the person's agency, (b) the capacity, condition, or state of acting or of exerting power, and finally, (c) a person or
thing through which power is extended or to which an end is achieved.
It is suggested here that the *type* of synthesizer used in a recording often
determines or limits an agent (the player *or* controller) and their decision-
making. Further to this, it's important to discuss the recognition and
utilisation of agency as a fundamental human quality, as it has the power
to direct and regulate the conditions of musicmaking. From analogue to
digital synthesis, the synthesizer's functionality is often contextualised by
technological change. Mayr continues:

> The defining characteristic of technology is its *functionality*, not its
> specific materiality. Technology, thus, (1) denotes those entities—
> artefacts, techniques, institutions, systems—that are or were func-
> tional and (2) emphasises the functional dimension of those entities.
> (Ibid., 1053)

This (brief) introduction to the areas of TD and agency allows us to highlight the aesthetical shaping of technology and the synthesizer, to give it
a context of how it was used by performers documented in the book.
These approaches also support the dialogue that exists between man and
machine, a conversation long-documented throughout in many musical
outputs, many of which are discussed in this book.

## AESTHETICAL FRAMEWORKS: CYBERNETICS

Cybernetics is a transdisciplinary approach for exploring regulatory systems—their structures, constraints, and possibilities. The term is often used in a rather loose way to imply the control of any system using technology or toward the scientific study of how humans, animals, and machines control and communicate with each other. It also opens up questions about technology and its unknown effects. Norbert Wiener, the so-called father of cybernetics, published *Cybernetics or Control and Communication in the Animal and the Machine* in 1948 and questioned the idea of progress, considering that 'progress imposes not only new possibilities for the future but new restrictions' (Wiener 1948, 46–47).

Cybernetic systems are used to model practically every phenomenon, with varying degrees of success—factories, societies, machines, ecosystems, brains. Later, Stafford Beer in *In the Brain of the Firm* (1972) provided a valuable insight into cybernetics' relationship to music and, for the purpose of this book, the synthesizer, in that, 'instead of trying to specify it (a system) in full detail, you specify it only somewhat. You then ride on the dynamics of the system in the direction you want it to go' (Beer 1972, 68–69).

One famous non-musician, Brian Eno, would go on to use cybernetics, linking its powerful toolset to the process of music composition. Its theories connect engineering, math, physics, biology, and psychology, and some of this inevitably trickled into the arts. A piece of music composed using feedback could be left to run; in turn, the system is the musician, not the player. Through this process, the musician can trust the synthesizer to make creative decisions.

## POPULAR CULTURE AND THE SYNTHESIZER

Tracing this history could take all manner of side roads and boundaries and could very well exist as a publication in its own right. With this in mind, a number of key elements and dates will be discussed. As discussed briefly, before the synthesizer, electronically generated sounds would come in the form of test equipment and banks of primitive oscillators and filter bands.

A conduit for the popularisation of electronically generated sounds in Britain is key to its rise: the medium of television and a group of composers and engineers who formed the BBC Radiophonic Workshop (1958–1998). One of its founding members, Daphne Oram, would go on to create music and special sound for BBC radio plays, including *Prometheus*

*Unbound* (1957), *Private Dreams and Public Nightmares* (1957), and *Amphitryon 38* (1958). Her experiments with electronically manipulated music can be traced to the late 1940s with her visionary *Still Point* (1948–1949), a work for two orchestras and a turntable soloist. Traditional compositional approaches contributed to her frustration with the Workshop's focus on dramatic scoring and sound design.

Two events are presented here toward the popularisation of synthesizer in Britain. Firstly, in November 1963, a major milestone would come from the Radiophonic Workshop, turning the nation on to sounds from beyond. The work, composed by Ron Grainer and realised by Delia Derbyshire at the radiophonic workshop, would become seminal in the creation of new sound worlds and moreso, its advent in the popularisation of electronically generated sound.

The theme song from *Dr. Who* (1963) was one of the first television themes to be created and produced by entirely electronic means. The synthesizer was unavailable at the time. Each note was created by cutting tape sections of a single plucked string. This was combined with the sounds of white noise and primitive oscillators and varying tape speed manipulations to create a composition whose sound would prove influential in the oncoming dominance of the synthesiser. Even though Grainer is credited as composer, Derbershire's work deserves so much more attention, as she was a pioneer of her era, working in a field and climate dominated by members of the other sex, who were often disapproving of her technical abilities.

Secondly, another television event within this (short) history is considered here, due to the effect it would have on many subjects within this book, including Cabaret Voltaire's Chris Watson and Throbbing Gristle's Chris Carter. The BBC's broadcast of Roxy Music's performance on the Old Grey Whistle Test on June 20, 1972, would go on to change popular musicmaking in Britain. Their radical approach to popular musicmaking, one that borrowed from that past and blundered the future, would go on to inspire countless acts in the mid- to late 1970s. The band opened with 'Ladytron' and began with a strange and atonal atmosphere, conducted by Andy McCay's clarinet being processed through Brian Eno's EMS VSC3 synthesizer. What then begins as a more traditional pop/rock song, in the end expands into a sound and sonic exploration never before heard from the BBC's Maida Vale studios. Roxy Music presented what would be an escape from the mundane reality, showcasing a mesh of pop nostalgia, off-the-beat rock music, and experimental electronic music, all beamed into millions of TV sets across the country.

After leaving Roxy Music in 1973, Brian Eno observed that during the 1970s, while popular music was seeking variety, it seemed a type of music was needed for an almost lack of variety, and through this he developed notions of a music that was 'part of the ambience of our lives—to be continuous, a surrounding.' His aim was to 'to immerse myself in sound, to make music to swim in, to float in, to get lost inside' (Eno, quoted in Cox & Warner 2004, 95). For the production of *Discrete Music* (1977), Eno used an EMS Synthi AKS (one that incorporated a digital sequencer). A portable modular analog synthesizer made by Electronic Music Systems of England, it was most notable for its patch pin matrix. Its functions and internal design, similar to the VCS3 synthesizer, were also made by EMS, and they would become more widely known on Pink Floyd's 'On the Run' from *The Dark Side of the Moon* (1973), via the use of the EMS Synthi.

The liner notes to *Discrete Music* borrows heavily from Beer's writings on cybernetics and provides a valuable insight to the process that sums up Eno's aesthetic and creative processes toward the synthesizer. He states:

> Since I have always preferred making plans to executing them, I have gravitated towards situations and systems that, once set into operation, could create music with little or no intervention on my part. That is to say, I tend towards the roles of the planner and programmer, and then become an audience to the results.[2]

Eno accepted himself, within the piece, as playing a passive role within the compositional process, and it seems the processes developed within the piece were developed over a ten-year period from first experimenting with tape recorders and echo machines. Further to this, Eno attempted to ignore the tendency to play the artist by dabbling and interfering within the production process. As the piece eventually turned out to be a piece of 'systems' music, and using cybernetics as a model, Eno felt it appropriate to develop a score, not in the traditional sense, but of an operational diagram. *Discrete Music* focuses on a perceptual process of the decay of an idea: The decay of a sound will loose and regenerate over time when it is played back, re-recorded, and played back over and over again, and the decay of the conceptual model was proposed by Eno from the outset. What we are presented with then is the gradual transformation of a recognizable musical phrase. The generation of such music(s) comes with many considerations. One contribution the album made was that of 'background music,' or what is at times more crassly referred to as 'elevator music.'

In *Noise: The Political Economy of Music*, Jacques Attali made the following observation about such music(s), in that:

> Ambiguous and fragile, ostensibly secondary and of minor importance, it has invaded our world and daily life. Today, it is unavoidable, as if, in a world now devoid of meaning, background noise was increasingly necessary to give people a sense of security. (Attalli 1985, 3)

Attali's point about music's apparent triviality is important; he remarks that:

> All music, any organisation of sounds is...a tool for the creation or consolidation of a community, of a totality. It is what links a power centre to its subjects, and thus, more generally, it is an attribute of power in all its forms...any theory of power today must include a theory of the localization of noise and its endowment with form...noise is inscribed from the start within the panoply of power. (Ibid., 6)

Attali's concepts relating to noise, music, and power are of particular relevance here. Eno verbalised and demonstrated a concept that perfectly fit its time and place and that has visibly shifted the landscape of musical thought, and by subjectively removing himself from the production process, he helped create a sense of space where there was once an object. In many ways, Eno utilised the synthesizer to create a utilitarian music, reduced, stripped of its fundamental cultural importance. Ultimately, this process led to a reconsideration and reevaluation of how the synthesizer is used, which via the BBC and the Old Grey Whistle Test, meant that many upcoming non-musicians now saw a new world and approach unfold before their eyes.


## CONCLUSION

The aesthetic frameworks presented here frame the synthesiser in terms of its usage and its influences on the creative process. In terms of the influence upon the artists in this publication, Eno's approach to the synthesizer was monumental, and his referencing to cybernetics resonated with a new generation of electronic musicians who sought new systems and theory for music production, one more based on free-roaming ideas rather than that of predetermined ones. As Punk appeared, the musician's mindset altered, as for some, the actual execution of music could now incorporate little or no intervention on the musician's part.

Current electronic music production methods offer the musician a creative utopia: access to unlimited possibilities, tonalities, and the total control over every imaginable parameter of sound. This type of control can leave the modern electronic music producer in somewhat of a void. Current computer platforms tend to have a very distinctive and recognisable sound palate, a sound palate that can, at times, lack sonic character. What these modern systems of music production (Abelton, Logic, Pro Tools) lack is that of the unknown, the unstable, something in which Eno and others revelled, which they explored and rebelled within during its heyday of the late 1970s in Britain. More interactive and tactile musicmaking platforms, such as Cycling 74's Max/MSP, certainly do open up 'generative' options for the electronic music musician, but again, surely the computer is the creative force, and the user is merely feeding it a chain of commands. Whilst current music technology does its best at reimagining the electronic instruments of the past, through physical modelling,[3] the process, creatively, is different, detached, and nowhere near immediate.

As Eno observes, it is what you *do* with these tools that is what matters, in that:

> The technologies we new use have tended to make creative jobs doable by many different people: new technologies have the tendency to replace skills with judgement–it's not what you can do that counts, but what you choose to do, and this invites everyone to start crossing boundaries. (Eno 1996, 394)

With a computer, a controlled form of interaction exists, although open source software allows some freedom from this. For the vast majority of electronic musicians today, the synthesizers once used by Eno and the acts documented here sell for extravagant sums of money, so the sound world they were (are) famed for generating is totally out of reach for many. Ultimately, via technological determinism, the computer drives the sound of electronic music today as it represents the most functional and economical way to produce it. However, this process also sees the loss of a more traditional means, which, in turn, influences the level of knowledge in our society about electronic musicmaking today.

## NOTES

1. The synthesizers used by the acts documented in this book were analogue synthesizers.

2. See liner notes to Brian Eno's *Discreet Music* (1977) EG/Virgin Records.

3. Physical modelling refers to sound synthesis methods in which the waveform of the sound to be generated is computed using a mathematical model, a set of equations and algorithms to simulate a physical source of sound, usually a musical instrument.

# II

# OUTSIDER ELECTRONICS

# 4

# CABARET VOLTAIRE

## Dadaism Up North

William Bell Scott's painting *Iron and Coal* (1855–1860) depicts a group of men working in an iron foundry, their arms raised in labour, using long-handled hammers to pound an object in the fire. In the lower portion sits a young girl; like others of her class and generation, she will benefit from the new prosperity brought by mining, engineering, and invention. The Industrial Revolution (1760–1840) firmly established Northern England as a powerhouse within this global maturity, and with the development of the free market (or the rise of capitalism), the rule of law,[1] and the benefits of colonialism, an unprecedented explosion of new ideas and new technological inventions came about that transformed the use of energy, creating an increasingly industrial and forward-minded nation.

Economic historian Robert Allen has argued that during this period, 'high wages, cheap capital and very cheap energy in Britain made it the ideal place for the industrial revolution to occur' (Allen 2010, 122), and now that capital was available for industrialists to invest in research and development, they expanded their knowledge base both in Britain and abroad, bringing about the rise and popularisation of intellectual property. Such modernisation and progress was not viewed as enlightening to all, including the poets of the Romantic Movement: William Blake, John Keats, Lord Byron, and Mary Shelley. Shelley's *Frankenstein (or The Modern Prometheus)* ponders and reflects upon whether or not progress—in particular, scientific progress—works against humanity rather than working in conjunction with it, as:

> Beware; for I am fearless, and therefore powerful. Life, although it may only be an accumulation of anguish, is dear to me, and I will defend it. (Shelley 1818, 133)

What overrides *Frankenstein* are the limits of science and technology, and this is reflected in every person whom the protagonist, Victor Frankenstein, had cared about, showing us that society should believe in the sanctity of human life and that the human mind should be wary of great and sudden change.

A modernist and brutalist systematic format of change was coming to the cities of northern Britain during the mid- to late 1970s, including the home of Cabaret Voltaire, Sheffield. This city was revamped during the 1970s, and its urban planning was a poster child for modernist futurescapes. Heavily targeted in the Blitz during World War II, on the nights of the 12th and 15th of December 1940, it was targeted by the Nazis due to the significance of its industral outputs, much of which had been turned to in the manufacturing of weapons and ammunition for the war effort.

The dominance of automation would see many of the key factories and industries come to be closed during the 1950s and 1960s. The development of housing projects like Park Hill Flats, built between 1957 and 1961, would come to represent the way forward for many cities up north. In order to accommodate such a population increase, many parts of the surrounding area were demolished to make way for a new system of roads. Given this, it would be incorrect to assume this geography directly shaped Stephen Mallinder, Richard H. Kirk, and Chris Watson's Cabaret Voltaire's outputs; it is perhaps more appropriate to postulate that the industrialization of the city, along with the social and authoritarian conditions that came with it, helped colour their sound. In a wider effect, laid-off workers and strikes helped further undermine the city's climate and social and cultural atmosphere. Such 'atmospheres' are explored in this chapter, presented through the early development and aesthetics of the band, the technology they used, and an analysis of their album *Mix Up* (1979).

## INFLUENCES

Dadaism was the ultimate European avant-garde art movement, one that challenged and rejected societal and cultural norms. From its beginning in a coffee shop in central Zurich, aptly named Cabaret Voltaire, it would go on to spur similar movements in New York (c. 1915), Paris (c. 1920), and Japan, Georgia, and Russia. In 1916, Hugo Ball, unwilling leader of the Dada movement, penned the first 'Dada Manifesto' in Zurich. This short but influential text highlighted Ball's opposition to Dada becoming an art movement in the first place and would go on to create conflict with the Dadaist circles, including Tristan Tzara. In line with Ball's manifesto,

Tzara would go on to publish his own manifesto and would similarly be as abstract and form a collection of thoughts, mostly against the very notion of a manifesto. He wrote:

> To put out a manifesto you must want: A. B. C. / fulminate against 1. 2. 3. / fly into a rage and sharpen your wings to conquer and disseminate little abcs and big abcs / sign, shout, swear, organise prose into a form of absolute and irrefutable evidence, to prove your *non plus ultra*. (Tzara 1918, 1)

Tzara considered art as both a serious conditional and at the same time, just a game, one that explores core traits of its movement. His writings were mostly inspired by both the contempt of bourgeois culture and toward more traditional viewpoints within art. Ultimately the differences of viewpoints within each manifesto would split options within the movement with Ball leaving Zurich for good in 1918.

Dadaism covered a wide range of art forms, including the visual, sculptrual, literary, sound, collage, and cutup writing techniques.[2] At heart, it was anti-capitalist and attempted to deconstruct the capitalist worldview by incorporating the nonsensical and irrational into art, and its home was a place where ideas could run freely, the neutrality of Switzerland. Influenced by Cubism, Expressionism, Futurism, and Constructivism, Dadaism looked to change the world, or at best, alter its view toward war, nationalism, and class systems. Again, the manifestos attempted to consider and address these issues. The collective would go on to include the artists Jean Arp and Emmy Hennings (Hugo Ball's wife and cofounder of Cabaret Voltaire), and they were perhaps the first anarchists in art, a movement that was apocalyptic in their collective approaches in which it anticipates 'an imminent cosmic cataclysm in which God destroys the ruling powers of evil and raises the righteous to life in a messianic kingdom.'[3]

More musical streams of Dadaist works came primarily from the work of the artist Kurt Schwitter (1887–1948), who developed the concept of *sound-poems*. After falling out with the Berlin-based Dadaists, Schwitter would go on to form his own group, *Merz*. First performed on the 4th of February 1925 at the home of Irmgard Kiepenheuer in Potsdam, *Ursonate* (1922–1932) uses two *Plakatgedichte* (Poster Poems) by Raoul Hausmann, which provided the sonata's opening line: 'Fumms bö wö tää zää Uu, pögiff, kwii Ee.' It consists of four movements: *Erster Teil*, *Largo*, *Scherzo*, and *Presto*.

Dutch composer and vocalist Jaap Blonk, who has both performed and recorded the piece, observed that:

> Somehow Schwitters, as in much of his visual art, managed to find the right balance between quasi-naïve freshness and strong structure. The piece is very much founded in the directness of real life, and still is great art at the same time. (Blonk 2009, 4)

The piece would go on to influence modern art and music, including Eno's incorporation of *Ursonate* in 'Kurt's Rejoiner' from *Before and After Science* (1977). Dadaism's legacy can be seen right across the arts, in multiple offshoots; in the early 1920s, it would go on to have a major influence on the development of the surrealist movement in Paris, another point of reference within Cabaret Voltaire's canon of aesthetics. With the onset of World War II and Adolf Hitler's attitudes toward what was referenced as 'degenerate art,' many of the Dadaists immigrated to the United States, and although less active as an art movement, Dadaism would go on to influence core upcoming American art movements, including modernism, and literature.

Cabaret Voltaire would go on to incorporate, in both compositional, performative arenas and artwork (covers, videos, promotional material), key techniques developed by Dadaism, which included:

**Collages:** Taken primarily from the Cubist movement, this process involves cutting up images and assembling them into art (*Double Vision* 1982).

**Cutup Technique:** Popularised by both William Burroughs and David Bowie, this involved cutting up words to reconstruct more chance-like narratives (*Voice of America* 1980).

**Photomontage:** This involves the use of scissors and glue rather than paintbrushes and paints to express views of modern life through images presented by the media (*Drinking Gasolene* 1985).

**Assemblage:** This involved the assembly of everyday objects to produce meaningful or meaningless pieces of work (across their discography via the use of homemade electronic devices).

One more movement within the arts would go on to influence, more directly, the narrative of Cabaret Voltaire: Situationist International. Most active between 1957–1972 in Europe and assembled from, amongst others, past members of the Dadaist and Surrealist movements, the foundational approach here was the idea of 'the spectacle.' The spectacle was a unified critique of advanced capitalism and the increasing tendency toward the expression and mediation of social relations through objects. Artists took this theory, first proposed by Guy Debord in his book *The Society of the Spectacle* (1967),[4] out of the art galleries and into the streets and communities, via the construction of situations, moments of life deliberately constructed for the purpose of the liberation of everyday life.

Cabaret Voltaire would embrace the movement's approach during their early beginnings, as Sheffield music historian Martin Lilleker observed and reposed that, the 'band would drive around town blasting Sheffield's own sounds from their speakers mounted on top of a friend's van. They would jump out of cars to play high-volume tale loops at the city's unsuspecting pedestrians.'[5] Situationist International would also influence Factory Records band the Durutti Column, which took its name from artist André Bertrand's collage *Le Retour de la Colonne Durutti*.[6] At heart, the movement was anarchic in that their ideas played an important role in the revolutionary events in Paris during 1968.

In Sheffield, Cabaret Voltaire made cultural productions, a part of everyday life, and it's fitting that their studio, Western Works, would be housed in what was once a World War II air shelter. Their own experimental recording studio would feature as a key focal point in Sheffield's musical community, recording demos and early works of acts such as Clock DVA. Such an environment embodies, at heart, core values to the Situationist International movement, in that the production of commodities was an end to itself and production by way of survival.

## BEGINNING(S)

Hegarty (2007) observes that the sociopolitical implications of Industrial music is both reflective and comparative of life, in that:

> Industrial music plays out the accursed share of modern society, staging sacrificial performances and making music that offers momentary collapse of rational thought in the shape of a listening that would know in advance what it would be listening to. (Heggarty 2007, 105)

Cabaret Voltaire used technology to shrink the distance between them and cities like London and penned the way for other seminal Sheffield bands like the Human League, and in later eras, Pulp and the establishment of

Warp Records. In a similar vein to Throbbing Gristle, Cabaret Voltaire shared their in-house vision through self-produced art and studio spaces.

Initially operating outside the music industry (although signing later to Mute and Virgin Records), Stephen Mallinder, Richard H. Kirk, and Chris Watson operated outside the bounds of traditionalism. Core to the early development of the band was Watson, who shared similar interests with Throbbing Gristles, and Chris Carter, in the building and designing of electronic instruments or using nontraditional methodologies to make electronic music, as Watson describes:

> We were all interested in the non-musical side initially—but that was my main contribution throughout my time with the group. My contribution was not through a particular instrument as it was with the other two—Richard with the guitar and wind instruments and Mal with the bass, percussion and voice. I was more concerned with sounds in general and in the production of records. I worked more as an engineer of sounds rather than actually playing an instrument to produce them. (Watson quoted in Reed 2013, 216)

Eno was another point of departure for Watson, along with the vast majority of nonconformist electronic musicians in Britain during the mid-1970s. From what began as a purely experimental sound project, Cabaret Voltaire would go on to take these techniques and turn them into full-fledged outputs and later, ones that would become quite successful with *Nag Nag Nag* (1979), which sold quite well in continental Europe.

Beginning in Watson's family home, the trio, in order to exploit the latest electronic music technologies available at the time, somehow managed to convince the upper management of the music department of Sheffield University to use their electronic music studio, which housed an EMS VCS3 synthesizer. Eno's workhorse, it 'obviously it appealed to us because Eno used a VCS3—however the idea of using a very technical synthesizer rather than a keyboard based one was very appealing to us. Those were the only instruments we had access to' (Mallinder 2020, 206). Indeed, the initial setup of the band was nonconformist, nontraditionalist, and anarchic, in that:

> We started working in Chris's loft with only tape recorders and a few things to bang as percussion. However, the first instrument we bought was an AKS, which was a suitcase synthesizer—again it was a non-musician type of synthesizer, more of a sound generator. I suppose the next thing that was an indicator as to the way we would develop, was that Richard bought a clarinet for about 15 pounds. Then

a few months later, it was Richard's birthday and Chris bought him a guitar for 5 pounds. (Ibid., 206)

Their early approaches to sound generation would lead to a mix of sonic elements, both electronic and acoustic, but also a core element of Eno's approach: the processing of acoustic sounds, electronically. Much the same as Throbbing Gristle, the band's early work was outputted on cassette tape, with Eno apparently receiving the first one.[7] Much of these early tape recordings would go on to feature on *Methodology: '74—'78 Attic Tapes*, released on Mute Records in 2019.

Their early performances were visceral at the core as they were in many ways, 'composition in real time,' incorporating elements within the intersection of technology, Punk, Dadaism, and music. Mallinder, who would bring the vocal element to the group, is perhaps the band's most important element. As much of the band's vocal presentation is processed, it becomes detached, floated around the steady beat of a drum machine. Such a process allowed Mallinder to become an auditory nonconformist; here now the traditional role of the lead singer was gone, and its replacement was an attention-grabbing 'nag.'

During the late 1970s, many independent UK studios became associated with either labels or bands associated with the label, the most famous being Factory Records' alliance with engineer Martin Hannet and Cargo Recordings Studios in Rochdale, Greater Manchester. In 1977, Watson financed the establishment of the band's own recording studio on the second floor of a building called the Western Works on Portobello Street, Sheffield. As previously discussed, it served as the band's studio for many years, as well as providing a social gathering spot for the local Sheffield scene. Having a non-commercial, exploitory space in which to experiment with sound at its very core was elemental for not only Cabaret Volatire's developing sound, but the same can be said of nearly all the acts discussed in this book.

Given the artistic isolation of the city to places like London, although greatly improved by the building of the A1 motorway in 1964, in many ways the group had to be the liberitat, to go on and serve the greater good, to be anarchic in all aspects of their approach, and without it, early acts like Clock DVA, the Future, the Human League, and ABC. What is highlighted here is the importance and significance of the urban experience and/or the set of aesthetics or values that a communal space can bring to a musical community, one that, in this case, broke down traditional ideologies toward both musicmaking and its production.

First published in 1964 and still in circulation today, *Practical Electronics* would become a milestone in the development of both musicians and nonmusicians' growing interest in home electronics. Both Chris Carter and Chris Watson would use their engineering backgrounds and technical ability to further extend both of the bands' sound (Carter's *Grizzilizer* is discussed further in chapter 5). This was Punk aesthetics at its core; building from scratch, sound and sonic devices that would go on to inform and influence the group's output.

A contributor to *Practical Electronics* was F.C. Judd. Known for his work primarily within amature radio, he would go on to inform and be part of early British electronic musicmaking. After serving in the forces during World War II, he trained as an engineer and soon saw the possibilities electronics offered toward sound and musicmaking. Along with Daphne Oram (BBC Radiophonic workshop cofounder), he was enthusiastically promoting electronic music to the British public via demonstrations and lectures to amateur tape-recording clubs and much of his technical knowledge would go on to be published as *Electronic Music and Musique Concrete* (1961). In the absence of any interest from the world of music, Judd was a true Punk; he worked completely outside the music community in the 1950s and 1960s. His only infiltration into the popular zeitgeist, Judd made TV soundtracks, including *Space Patrol* (1963), which was the first British TV series to have a fully electronic score.[8] In a similar vein to what was occurring in Western Works, Judd made the score using tape manipulation, loops, and tone generators in his home studio in London.

Following a belated and long-overdue recognition of early British electronic-music composers like Tristram Cary, Daphne Oram, and Delia and Derbyshire, Judd's work was reworked by a collection of composers and producers (including TG's Chris Carter) on London's Public Information label entitled *Electronics Without Tears* (2012).

In 2011, Judd was the focus of *Practical Electronica*, an experimental documentary by director Ian Helliwell, which allowed a whole new generation of electronic musicmakers. Judd was also seminal in both publishing and working on a rather specialised community of *Amature Tape Recording* (ATR) magazine. Launched in 1959 and later rebranded as *Studio Sound* in 1970, the magazine would go on to become a seminal publication, much the same as *Practical Electronics*, in the development of a prototype DIY and underground movement, spurring people to, like others in this publication, take recording matters into their own hands. After his death in 1992 and after publishing eleven books ranging from tape recording, home recording, and amature electronics, Judd can be seen as a significant figure within the context of the acts discussed within this book.

Middleton (1990) laid out the conditions in which collective elements and environments encourage the production of works, much as to what Western Works would produce, commenting that 'most accounts of studio recording that we have suggest a great range of patterns, varying according to historical periods, social and institutional context, musical aims and individual motivations' (Middelton 1990, 91). Mallinder, Kirk, and Watson formed an institution of sorts with Western Works, in which the aesthetic processes of such a collaborative space brought about a form of artistic autonomy in which each member became creator, producer, engineer, and musician, and as Benjamin suggests, these forms of working could bring about not only democratisation, but new hierarchies in that 'the auteur remains, merely changing his position and identity' (Ibid., 91).

It's difficult to quantify the output from Western Works, but the popular record-selling website discogs.org lists some 362 releases[9] to its name, which makes it one of the most prolific independent studios in Britain during its operation.

Later, the production of *Red Mecca* (1981) and *The Crackdown* (1983), part Some Bizzare/Virgin Records, would see recordings take place in London, and the further they got from Western Works, it would seem the group (along with Watson departure in 1981) distanced itself further from its industrial origins, toward a more commercial sound. The demolition of Western Works in 1987 would ultimately see further reliance on London as a conduit for the band.

## THE AGE OF NOISE: *MIX-UP* (1979)

Noise, considered by many as unwanted, and mistakenly defined as such by some, has little respectability and conjures up images of rejection, the unwanted. Yet, its rise since the advent of the postindustrial society means that, as the world grows larger, the noise gets louder, or as writer Aldous Huxley defined it:

> The twentieth century is, among other things, the age of noise. Physical noise, mental noise and noise of desire—we hold history's record for all of them. And no wonder; for all the resources of our almost miraculous technology have been thrown into the current assault against silence. (Huxley 1970, 218)

The history of noise is fascinating, beginning with Einstein's explanation of Brownian motion. In a nutshell, it is the random motion of particles suspended in a medium (gas, liquids), named after botanist Robert

Brown. He discovered the process while looking through a microscope at the pollen of the plant *Clarkia Pulchella* immersed in water. It was Einstein who then used Brown's discovery and modelled the motion of the pollen particles as being moved by individual water molecules, making one of his first major scientific contributions: that noise could establish the existence of atoms.

In music, noise provides an erratic acoustic vibration that is intermittent or statistically aleatory or 'any auditory sensation which is disagreeable or uncomfortable' (Burns 1969, 14), and historically, it was in use in Western music across a number of genres, from the Italian Futurists composer Luigi Rossollo to twentieth-century classical music composers, including György Ligeti.

Hegarty (2007) observes that 'noise is not an objective fact. It occurs in relation to perception—both direct (sensory) and according to presumptions made by the individual. These are going to vary according to historical, geographical and cultural location' (Hegarty 2007, 3). Such conditions surrounded Western Works, surrounded Mallinder, Kirk, and Watson, and to understand, or to gain perspective on the significance of noise, in both the arts and sciences, is to understand Cabaret Voltaire's 1979 album *Mix-Up*.

Jacques Attali's *Noise: The Political Economy of Music* presents concepts relating to noise and music and are of particular relevance here; in that music, a supposedly pleasurable and emotionally expressive force is not neutral, but is (as with the rest of the products of the entertainment industry) politically aligned, in that:

> All music, any organisation of sounds is...a tool for the creation or con-solidation of a community, of a totality. It is what links a power centre to its subjects, and thus, more generally, it is an attribute of power in all its forms...any theory of power today must include a theory of the localization of noise and its endowment with form...noise is inscribed from the start within the panoply of power. (Attali 1985, 6)

Attali viewed the evolution of music under a number of stages, which included Sacrificing, Representing, Repeating, and Post-Repeating[10] Moreso, these cultural structures allow for music's transmission and reception. For example, 'sacrificing' defines music as ritualised, and 'post-repeating' points more toward both sampling and electronic music and its manipulation possibilities. Ultimately, each stage carries with it a certain set of technologies for producing, recording, and disseminating music. The making of Cabaret Voltaire's *Mix-Up* reflects Attali's thesis that music, as a cultural form, is tied up in the mode of production in any given society.

After Throbbing Gristle offered to release their debut album on Industrial Records, funds were unavailable at the time, and on their recommendation, the band signed to Rough Trade in early 1978. Their earliest recordings were primarily circulated within mail art communities (via Kirk), some of which would eventually appear on *Methodology 74/78 Attic Tape* (2002). *Extended Play EP* (1978) was their first release on the label, and it featured the live classic 'Do the Mussolini-Headkick' and a version of 'Here She Comes Now' by the Velvet Underground.

The single 'Nag Nag Nag' (June 1979) would go on to have greater traction, selling upwards of ten thousand copies, including quite a significant number in France and Belgium. The track is in many ways a throwback to 1960s garage punk, washed with fuzz tones and a pulsating Farfisa organ throughout. Heavy noise and distortion run through the track, which decentralises Mallinder's voice or presence as the lead vocalist and part of the tracks 'nagging factor' is, indeed, noise in the form of 'a constant 1300 Hz sizzle that runs through its electronic timbres that sounds more like a dental suction tool than a synth or guitar' (Reed 203, 64). Despite poor reviews, some glowing and positive ones did appear, most notably from Andy Gill of the NME, who wrote that he 'firmly believed Cabaret Voltaire will turn out to be one of the most important new bands to achieve wider recognition this year. Wait and see.'[11]

Even at this stage, the sound of the three members was formed: Watson's synth processing, Mallinder's pulsating bass, and Kirk's stabbing, angular guitar lines. This sound world would continue to prevail throughout 1977–1979 and until 1982, when a more commercial approach was dominant. Nevertheless, what would remain was the aesthetic and attitudes of the band, and even with Watson's departure, Reynolds in 'Rip It Up' and 'Start Again' eloquently describes their approach in that 'they blended a Yorkshire-bred bloody minded intransigence in the face of badge-holders and bureaucrats with the sort of pot-filled never met a conspiracy theory I didn't like; attitude you found throughout squatland' (Reynolds 2001, 171).

Released on October 23, 1979, on Rough Trade, *Mix-Up* builds on the success of 'Nag Nag Nag' and presents a mode of production that sets the band mark of both industrial and post-Punk genres. 'Kirlian Photograph' opens the album. Its title is apt: It was named after Semyon Kirlian, who, in 1939, accidentally discovered that if an object on a photographic plate is connected to a high-voltage source, an image is produced. Abrasive and dissonant electronics cloud the mix that is supported by a primitive drum machine (either a Farfisa or Selmer) and wandering bassline. The noise bursts used throughout are these 'kirlian' high-voltage sources, moving back and forward, aggravating both the song and perhaps its listener. Right from the beginning, the band is using noise as a weapon, a mode that is either disagreeable or uncomfortable to the listener, depending on the listener's taste, of course.

This approach was used to sway both the listeners and its range of potential commercial success, as Kirk points toward in this 2013 interview, commenting:

> We definitely retained a darker, more subversive side to what we were doing, but we definitely wanted to reach more people. If we made something darker, the beats would hold it together. It wasn't any kind of formal decision, it just seemed natural. We'd been big fans of dance music in the 70s but it was the technology that was the missing link. Suddenly we got programmable drum machines and sequencers, and with that we got the repetition you need for dance music—it brought that sound within our grasp.[12]

'No Escape' follows the approach of 'Nag Nag Nag': fuzzed-out garage rock. Written by Richard Elvern Marsh in 1965 and performed by the Seeds, it is an interesting cover version. Appearing on the Seeds' 1966 album *The Seeds*, it is clean, upbeat, and full of energy, due to the band's appearances in and around Los Angeles clubs. Seventy-five hundred miles away, its reinterpretation has similar energies while it is washed in noise and a plulasting farfisa organ. The pounding drum machine, its lyrical detail 'nowhere to hide,' perhaps reflects the surrounding sociopolitical climate during this period of its history in Britain; secondly, toward the group's attitude toward paranoia of law, governmental, societal element. Mallinder has commented on such in the past, in that 'being in a state of paranoia is a very healthy state to be in. It gives you a permanently questioning and searching nonacceptance of the situation.'[13] In terms of references, the track very much is a nod toward Suicide, New York–based masters of minimalist electronics, pulsating rhythms, and confrontational live shows.

'Fourth Shot' begins with alien electronic textures, courtesy of Watson, that resemble something like a BBC radiophonic workshop. Kirk's fuzzed-out guitars dominate the foreground, sustaining elongated notes while Mallinder takes a more contemporary and 'melodic' approach to the song. Within this cacophony of instruments, the trio pull off what can only be described as a spell-burning wash of cross-referencing; King Tubby, Can, and Pierre Schaeffer all exist here, albeit within the group's own visionary approach. 'Heaven and Hell' follows with a wash of white noise and an electronic pulse reminiscent of a distant radio transmission.

Again, as if some sort of reprise, Kirk's distorted guitar populates. Polluted, this seems like a good analogy here; although mechanical, it's a miserable landscape.

This is further made evident with the introduction of Mallinder's vocals, aggravated and (lyrically) indistinguishable, with only words and phrases like 'mesclun haze' and 'senseless rejection' appearing from the mist. As the proto drum machine begins to accelerate in tempo, a real sense of continuity in sound and timbre now begins to appear, that of Kirk's distinct guitar sound, one that would continue through most of their catalogue.

What it presents is fragile, delicate, and confused. This is further pushed around in the soundscape by effects such as reverb, while the instruments are processed by Watson, perhaps on the EMS VCS3 from Sheffield University's Music Department. It's both alien and afraid, both coherent and incoherent. As the song ends, Mallinder is, in many ways, caught between this flux, as he screams both 'Heaven' and 'Hell,' and with this, 'he is no longer a singer in the band, not merely an implicit radical megaphone, but part of an aggravation machine, turned equally on its audience and itself' (Reed 2013, 64).

'Eyeless Sight' is the only live contribution to the album. It's an extended improvisation, and what is core to this is this: The inclusion of this on the album puts the listener in the audience's position. Intercut with vocal samples, it's a surrealist landscape, in a nod to both Brion Bysion and William Burroughs, both of whom were of major influence, in particular to Kirk.

It's a fantastic slice of *through the looking glass*, composition in real time and the inclusion of 'Eyeless Sight' is a great example of some of the group's core aesthetics: that of disruption and reaction techniques, further sighting Dadaism. Tristan Tzara, in the *Dada Manifesto* (1918), describes the construction of the cutup:

TO MAKE A DADAIST POEM
The poem will resemble you.
And there you are—an infinitely original author of charming sensibility, even though unappreciated by the vulgar herd.[14]

'Photophobia' is more akin to some of the frightening public service television commercial's line 'Protect & Survive.'[15] Produced in Britain during the late 1970s, it documents a nuclear fallout and remains a stark reminder of what the conditions of the Cold War brought about. In a blurred-out dub-like environment, Mallinder's spoken-word contributions are very much situationist and Dadais with memorable lines, singing: 'If the Rolling

Stones could not play the queen's music, they would be removed from the country.'

Kirk's guitar (processed by Watson) buzzes around, like a fly you're trying to swat while an underlying drone acts as a bed in which the madness unfolds. Bass guitar and drum machine soon follow, stumbling and gasping for air in what can only be described as a schizophrenia in sound. However, in terms of atmospherics, it's a standout contribution. Its slow motion bass line and drone make it a hypnotic listening process, and with the addition of these melodic elements, it allows the listener to remain in limbo. Although very much spiky and aggressive, halfway through the album at this stage, it remains engaged and totally accessible.

Studio drums, courtesy of Haydn Boyes Weston, a session drummer who would go on to session for other Sheffield mainplayers including the Human League and Heaven 17, appears on 'On Every Other Street.' The drum pattern (and its echo effects) sounds strangely like Talking Heads' 'Warning Sign' from their 1977 album, *More Songs About Buildings and Food*. As with the other contributions within the album, Kirk's processed-guitar stabs demand the attention space, while the flanger and delay create a dub-like soundspace. Mallinder's 'Da Da Da Da' lyric contributions populate the mix, and thematic continuities remain, a distrust for both pleasing melodic and rhythmic cohesion. 'Expect Nothing' features a drum machine (what sounds like a Korg Mini Pops) that dominates the foreground, which then becomes processed. The bass and guitar seems to play, somewhat in sync, but Watson's wash of electronics distorts this at times. Lyrical detail is, again, obscured. The piece ends on an electronic bed of noise as if suffocating from the torment induced.

'Capsules' ends the album, and it is fitting. Brittle and sparse, it bookends *Mix-Up* perfectly. Processing by Watson in many ways dominates, more so than the instruments. There is a final addition here to the album's formula: angular/dissonant rhythm guitar, electronic effects, noise experimentation, and obscured lyrical presentation.

*Mix-Up* is, in many ways, a history lesson; its lack of variety, contrast, challenging, and dark sound world allow it to stand out as a significant contribution to British industrial music of the late 1970s, a sound that would go on to continue to influence across genres from Post-Punk, noise, and lo-fi. In a world of digital music production, *Mix-Up* remains (sonically) dark, murky, and obscure, yet this distinct quality, which is both detrimental to its sound and could and perhaps repel the listener, is very much the defining part of the album's appeal.

## TECHNOLOGY

Cabaret Voltaire initially made the use of homemade electronics, which was, in many ways, made due to financial reasons. Watson used his engineering background to facilitate the band with rudimentary instruments and processing powers. It was Watson who was experimenting with tape decks in his parents' house in the Sheffield suburb of Totley in the early 1970s while Kirk built oscillators from mail-order kits.

When they came together, it was more about experimentation rather than musicmaking or a means of making music to either sell or perform it. Moreso, the process here at the beginning of the group was directed toward the exploration of sound rather than creating something more formal or structured.

As the group evolved, more traditional instruments were added to the mix; these included the clarinet and guitar. However, these instruments are often treated electronically. It would be Brian Eno who again would prove to be influential on Watson, not so much on his music, but more so on his process and approach to musicmaking, as Watson explains:

> Early Roxy Music for us was probably one of the sparks for the group. I remember seeing them in early 1972 at a college in Sheffield. I was completely knocked out, it actually changed my aspect on virtually everything I did regarding music both listening and production. I was interested in Brian Eno's technique and some of the sounds he produced. I learnt a lot about contemporary music through that, whereas my interest before that had come from the classic avant-garde such as Stockhausen, Schaeffer, Satie. (Watson quoted in Reed 2013, 216)

In terms of synthesizers and keyboards, the group would go on to use an endless line of electronic devices through each album. However, for the purpose of this discussion, only the early technological development of the group will be reviewed here. As previously mentioned, the group gained access to the University of Sheffield's Music Departments EMS VCS3, an instrument that would have been very much out of reach, financially, to any group of the 1970s, apart from the likes of Richard Wright (Pink Floyd) and ELP. Further to this, an EMS Synthi AKS Synthesizer was used by the group. More of a sound generator than a traditional synthesizer, it was Eno's go-to machine during this period. The machine was used on 'Do the Mussolini (Head Kick),' 'The Set Up' from *Extended Play*, and 'No Escape' and 'Heaven and Hell' from *Mix-Up*.

Watson also utilised a Vox Continental organ, which can be heard on *Mix-Up*'s 'No Escape.' In the early days, it was primarily the tape machines that would prove most useful and Dadaist with tape loops and collages becoming some of their first explorations into technology with sound. Again, Watson's career and training as a telephone engineer meant he had the technical know-how to produce and self-build electronic instruments such as an oscillator, which would become core to the group's early work. A consideration in the early years of the band was rhythm. Initially facilitated by tape loops, soon the drum machine would come into play. The earliest used by the band were drum machines that were primarily used by organ players as accompaniment, notably the Selmer MR 101 (1972) and Farfisa R10 (1970).

In many ways, these machines would become the foundation on which the group could explore ideas, as Mallinder explains:

> The whole rhythmic side of things came about from banging anything that was around the loft at the time—pure percussion. Whatever sounded good, you hit it. Also we used a lot of tape loops, and although not percussive in themselves, the whole notion of the tape loop is based on repetition, and it therefore becomes a percussive pulse. Leading on from that, as another way of generating rhythm we bought a drum machine. What appealed to us was the idea of providing a faultless beat, a pulse behind what we were doing to link things together. We didn't really want to use a drummer at the time because we didn't want to be part of the 'rock music' tradition. In a lot of ways we wanted to parody that whole 'rock' tradition and integrate it into the basic idea of sound collage. We wanted to juxtapose different forms of music, such as the avant garage experimental tradition, with a parody of rock music. (Mallinder quoted in Fish 2002, 207)

In terms of audio documentation, a Revox Tape Machine (most likely an A-77) was used by the group from an early stage, including one at the University of Sheffield's Music Department. Again, Eno's influence comes into sight here as the A-77 was heavily used by Eno on numerous albums during this period, including his seminal LP with King Crimson guitarist Robert Fripp, *No Pussyfooting* (1977). So much so was the significance of how the group would go on to have ultimate control of how their material was recorded, the band would go on to sign with Rough Trade in 1978 (in lieu of an advance) for a four-track Revox tape machine; this machine would go on to become the primary recording device of Western Works.

The band's relationship with technology would ultimately change when Steveo Pearce of Some Bizzare Records leveraged a licensing deal with Virgin that secured the band a £50,000 advance for the production of *The Crackdown* (1983). Here, with the aid of the most cutting edge music technology available at the time, Cabaret Voltaire would now write music for the new decade. With this, the direction and aesthetic quality of the group changed, and with each consecutive album, including *The Covenant, The Sword and the Arm of the Lord* (1985), the sound of Western Works was very much left behind, and London (Mallinder's new base) would be the environment where the group would base its future directions in sound.

## CONCLUSION

In *Hit Factories: A Journey Through the Industrial Cities of British Pop*, Carl Whitney considers Sheffield, the city, characteristic of its sound, in that 'new technology demanded a different kind of musician, one of great technical ability whose skills tended towards the practical requirements of an engineer' (Whitney 2019, 120). The term 'engineer' here can be interpreted in a multitude of variations as the act was engineering as much an aesthetic and approach, rather than a more formal audio engineering process. As per the acts reviewed and discussed in this book, the Punk movement's ethos was very much begging the drive (technologically) to do it yourself.

Cabaret Voltaire produced challenging music for its time, in an era of social and economic turmoil, and although not directly political, the ambience they created in their recordings, primarily in 1979's *Mix Up*, was a sonic brutality unlike anything to come from Britain from that period.

Cabaret Voltaire (via Dadaism and Situationist approaches) were unclassifiable—not a single classification can be applied to their approach—and indeed, the term 'industrial' has historically been a point of contention for the act, as it is almost a cheap shot at defining their contribution to the field of electronic music production in Britain during the late 1970s. This can be best summed up by Mallinder himself, as he attempts to explain (and educate) the masses, commenting:

> A brief work of warning. I have to confess to a level of discomfort when the term industrial is put on me. As a musician and producer, who it would seem, has more than a passing flirtation with what the media and music consumers broadly label "industrial music," or "industrial beats"

I tend to bristle a little. As a founding member of Cabaret Voltaire, a group who hail from a northern British industrial city, it seems I can offer little defence, though. (Mallinder quoted in Reed 2013, XI)

Genres are constructed by external factors in the way in which music markets make them, as it's easy to commodify, categorise, and sell a product. For Cabaret Voltaire, Sheffield would come to define how others would classify their sound. However, the band did play along with this, as it seemed functional to do so. Reconsider for a moment the climate of the era, with Thatcherism, the threat of nuclear war, and energy shortages. Rather than feeling encased by this, Cabaret Voltaire used their instruments and electronic machines to transcend and move through the day-to-day reality of late 1970s Britain.

Ultimately, Kirk, Mallinder, and Watson used technology in the search of an idealised future, and the noise, distortion, and fuzz effects used by the group were perhaps employed to blur and subvert this future, as for many, it wasn't something particularly good to look forward to.

## NOTES

1. Authority and influence of law in society, especially when viewed as a constraint on individual and institutional behaviour, (hence) the principle whereby all members of a society (including those in government) are considered equally subject to publicly disclosed legal codes and processes.

2. See also https://www.writing.upenn.edu/~afilreis/88v/burroughs-cutup.html (accessed December 16, 2021).

3. See Tzara 1918, *Dada Manifesto*, 391.org (accessed December 16, 2021).

4. Primarily based on Marxist critical theory, Debord presents 221 short theses in the form of aphorisms, including 'mass media commodity fetishism' and 'comparasments between religion and marketing.'

5. Mallinder, quoted in S. Alexander Reed's *Assimilate*, 62.

6. See also https://www.theideaofthebook.com/pages/books/2 (accessed June 10, 2022).

7. Mallinder, quoted in Mick Fish's *Industrial Evolution*, 206. (accessed May 12, 2022).

8. See also https://www.imdb.com/title/tt0164289/ (accessed August 2022).

9. See also https://www.discogs.com/label/267832-Western-Works (accessed March 22, 2022).

10. See also Dana Polan's review of *Noise: The Political Economy of Music* by Jacques. Attali, *Substance*, Vol. 17, No. 3, Issue 57 (1988), 56–58, https://www.jstor.org/stable/i287882. (accessed July 1, 2022).

11. See also June 27, 1978 edition of NME (New Musical Express).

12. R.K. Kirk, 'Interview,' *Electricity Club Magazine*, https://www.electricity-club.co.uk/cabaret-voltaire-interview/ (accessed July 7, 2022).

13. See Reynolds (2005, 171).

14. See also T. Tzara (1920), *On Feeble Love and Bitter Love*—Dada Manifesto.

15. Produced by the British government between 1974 and 1980, Protect and Survive was intended to advise the public on how to protect themselves during a nuclear attack. Its controversial subject, its cultural impact was longer-lasting than most public information campaigns.

# 5

# THROBBING GRISTLE

## Music from the Death Factory

Performance art has many different facets—music, dance, fixed media, and improvisation—and it has always shared a link to experimental music performance. Firstly, both are primarily presented on a stage, and this process allows it to be viewed in real time by the audience. Secondly, from a voyeuristic perspective, the audience watches 'art in motion,' and through the process of improvisation, this is extended further as the performer(s) react, change, and modify a performance.

Throbbing Gristle began their life as an experimental performance art group, and the traits briefly discussed above would become core not only to their live performances but also to their recorded musical output. Core to the group's philosophy were confrontational approaches and provocative visual imagery. Like many of the acts discussed in the book, musically they used the synthesizer and homemade electronic devices as instruments of subversion. Simon Ford's full-length study of the group, *Wreckers of Civilization* (1999), paints a very accurate picture of the band and its approaches through the lives of its shapeshifting members, from the freak scene/beat 1960s into the hostile and dystopian climate of the late 1970s.

In the *Industrial Culture Handbook*, Jon Savage identifies and defines five aesthetic approaches within industrial musicmaking, including:

1. Organised autonomy
2. Access to information
3. The use of synthesizers and antimusic
4. Extramusical elements
5. Shock tactics.[1]

Throbbing Gristle encompassed all the above (and more) in their lifespan, the first era being 1976–1981, and it helped form an ideology that is still prevalent today in challenging and subversive underground electronic music across the globe. All members of the group had careers in their own right before assembling as a band. Chris Carter began his career as a bass player and later as a technician for television and home electronics hobbyists, while Peter Christopherson (Sleazy) worked as a graphic designer. However, in the midst of the Punk movement, it would be Genesis P-Orridge (Neil Andrew Megson) and Cosey Fanni Tutti (Christine Carol Newby) whose platform of expression, via surrealist musical and theatrical happenings, would provide an aesthetic approach for the band to follow. This chapter presents the early development and aesthetics of the band and an analysis of their album *20 Jazz Funk Greats* (1979) via the use of the synthesizer and electronics.

## INFLUENCES

The Vienna Actionists[2] was an art movement between the mid-1960s and 1970s that explored many different fields, including improvisation and the reinterpretation of theatrical works, and their commune/art group environment was the breeding ground for artists who sought to break down the barriers between audience and performer. Artists including Hermann Nitsch and Otto Muhl used approaches close to the Fluxus movement to create real-time performances or 'happenings.' Moreso, the movement used the body as a performance mechanism that was often steeped in violence and destruction. Indeed, they sought to provoke moral panic through their work, with Muhl's work often leading to an arrest and fleeing for his safety, most famously for his piece *Piss Action* in 1968 Munich.

Much of their work would go on to inspire a young Neil Andrew Megson. After dropping out of university, Megson's involvement with Islington's Transmedia Explorations would be seminal in the foundation of COUM Transmissions.

Transmedia Explorations' unconventional approach to everyday life was influential; members could not sleep in the same location on consecutive nights, money was held in a central deposit, and clothes were changed daily in order to alter role and persona: a new costume on the daily stage of life. Under such social and living conditions, things were bound to break, and Megson's stay was only three months long, or perhaps it was the 'realisation that the hippie movement had fizzled, failing to deliver on its promise of radical change' (P-Orridge quoted Reed 2013, 75).

On his return to Hull, and renaming himself Genesis P-Orridge, a message came to him during a vision, aptly in his parents' house, in which he heard the words 'COUM Transmissions,' and he visualised the band's symbols of a semierect penis bearing the letters *COUM*, beneath which was the phrase 'YOUR LOCAL DIRTY BANNED.' Northern England would be the location for the first iterations for the COUM Transmissions' early experiments during 1971–1973, and after performing at a number of 'happenings,' the group began to attract some notoriety and were banned from most local venues. Bored with traditional approaches, P-Orridge and friend John Shapeero formed a collective that operated throughout the United Kingdom from 1969 to 1976 and was the grounding for Throbbing Gristle, as it also contained one of its founding members, Cosey Fanni Tutti, along with a wider circle of contributors.[3]

COUM Transmissions set out to challenge boundaries and conventions by using both confrontation and subversion as key elements of its approach. Primarily influenced by a greater disregard for the establishment,[32] they stared aspects of British society in the face, challenged them, and questioned them. The development and widespread use of the Pill, and even something as trivial as the miniskirt, was altering Britain in more ways than it perhaps cared for. Further to this, changing attitudes in society, divorce, abortion, and the 1967 legilization of homosexuality was used by P-Orridge to develop the group's aesthetics, spurred on by the increasing counterculture movement happening across the pond.

The wave of late-1960s experiments in music in Britain would be a influence on the collective, primarily on Tutti, commenting:

> The philosophical approach to music of Cornelius Cardew, Keith Rowe, Lawrence Sheaff, Lou Gare and Eddie Provost proved to be very influential and reads rather like an early version of what was to become COUM's approach to music: anti-harmony, no prerequisite for anyone to be able to play an instrument, and the sound the 'group' generated was also regarded as a contributory member of the group itself. (Tutti 2017, 78)

It was at Oval House in Kennington, South London, that the staging of the piece 'Couming of Age' (1974) would prove fruitful to the formation of Throbbing Gristle. Peter Christopherson approached P-Orridge and Tutti after the performance and was very much interested in the sexual nature of the performance; hence the 'sleazy' moniker was born.[33] More importantly,

Christopherson's employment at the time, at the seminal design company Hipgnosis,[34] led to COUM gaining access to cutting-edge computers and printing facilities, much of which would go on to be employed during the development and subsequent performance of their first collaborative piece, 'Couming of Youth,' first staged at the Melkweg, Amsterdam, in 1975. Sleazy's contribution to COUM made 'the three of us together made for a volatile mix, encouraging each other to indulge in our sexual interests and explorations and putting them center stage' (Ibid., 166).

Chris Carter would soon be introduced to the group via the visual artist John Lacey. At the time, he was touring universities and colleges with a solo multimedia show, and after having worked as a sound engineer at Granada, Themes Television, and the BBC, Carter's interest in self-built synthesizers and keyboards was becoming more prominent.

It would be COUM Transmissions' 1976 show, *Prostitution*, at London's ICA (Institute of Contemporary Arts), would prove to be the group's last major show and its most controversial. Based around Tutti's pornographic career to date, the show incorporated, amongst other things, rusty knives, syringes, tampons in a glass case, and a stripper. In a direct and mediated act of confrontation, Punks and prostitutes were hired to 'engage' with the audience. In the view of Andy Warhol's *Plastic Exploding Inevitable*, the show was a multimedia performance with performances from the Punk band Chelsea and Throbbing Gristle (the house band). The show would go on to catch the attention of the UK tabloid press, and in a hilarious turn of events, Tutti would reincorporate the press clippings back into the show. In a further turn of events, Scottish conservative MP Sir Nicholas Fairbairn summoned, from Arts Minister Harold Lever, an explanation into these so-called perverted events, labelling them as 'wreckers of civilization.'[4] This kind of press was key to the band's legacy, with the British performance and experimental music movement, and the COUM Transmissions' performances during the 1970s, firmly establishing the experimental performance art in Britain, and through the aid of the art council's support, they would go on to perform in Europe and the United States.

Even though *Prostitution* was COUM Transmissions' swan song, its reincarnation was transferred more directly to sonic experiments, via the formation of Throbbing Gristle. Tutti was keen to challenge both audience and listener, in that:

> We wanted a sound that hit people between the eyes and swirled in grinding, growling mayhem between their ears. A sound that caused an involuntary physical response in the body that would make people

feel and think rather than just listen, dance and get drunk. In the studio, we experimented with extreme frequencies; one of us stood at the 'kill switch' to cut the power if the effects became too much. We experience tunnel vision, our stomachs going into spasm and our trouser legs flapping. (Ibid., 241)

Without the formation of COUM Transmissions, the group would not have existed, and as elements like propaganda and pseudo-fascist iconography were carried over, most notably confrontationally performative elements such as the ones employed in songs like 'Discipline' (1977).

## BEGINNING(S)

Exploring the worlds of confrontation and subversion, the group now used musical instruments to channel and birth a music that was both dynamic and challenging. One only has to examine the kinds of music being produced in Britain during 1975—it was hardly inspirational. Bay City Rollers, Wings, and Rod Stewart were topping the charts. Perhaps it was of no or little influence or significance to Throbbing Gristle, if only its effect on the course of popular music at the time in Britain. Mike Oldfield's *Tubular Bells* was number nine in the bestselling albums of 1975. An album of purely instrumental sounds, the production's sonic productions (the use of synthesizers, tape echo, long reverberant sound) did allow it to stick out within the contemporary radio landscape soundscape. Although not infiltrating the underground electronic music scene at the time, it is nevertheless worth pondering whether this sound was subconsciously deepening the nation's consciousness to alternative approaches to musicmaking.

Another album worth noting, released at the cusp of the formation of Throbbing Gristle, was an album that would have very much informed the electronic sound of the group, in particular Chris Carter. *Rubycon* by Tangerine Dream was released by Virgin, and although it did not quite match the sales figures for *Phaedra* (1974), it nevertheless reached number ten in a fourteen-week run, their highest-charting album in the UK.

Recorded at the Manor Studio in Oxfordshire, owned at the time by Virgin Boss Richard Branson, the album used an array of influences and, indeed, machines, from choral and pastoral elements added to the impression that Froese, Franke, and Baumann had really absorbed the innovations of Stockhausen and Ligeti decades before. On the equipment front, Franke added a modified Elka organ, while Baumann introduced prepared piano and ARP synth. Edgar Froese remembers the recording, in that 'unlike *Phaedra*, there were no breaks in creative flow. The sequencers could now be technically better equipped, although many of the technical alterations had to be custom-built.'[5]

The chasm that separates Throbbing Gristle, Mike Oldfield, and Tangerine Dream is indeed wide. With the latter being very much about the control, refinement, and mastery of walls of modular synthesizers, the album is simply a refinement of its predecessor. Like many of the acts observed in this book, electronic music from Germany at the time was a considerable influence. Krautrock or Kosmische[6] music's influence on Carter is very much evident and is discussed later through in Carter's use of synthesised arpeggios, programmed on 'Walkabout' from *20 Jazz Funk Greats* (1979).

Core to the group's sonic approach was the use of prerecorded tape-based samples, highly distorted background, and spoken-word performances by Cosey Fanni Tutti or Genesis P-Orridge. These are all found on the group's debut single, *United / Zyklon B Zombie*, released on the band's own Industrial Records in May 1978. Not only is the single title a statement, as Zyklon B was a gas used by Nazi Germany during the Holocaust, but the artwork is just as controversial; the front and back covers provoke the above with a shower scene, cold and dark buildings.

*United/Zyklon B Zombie*'s sound world is stark, surreal, and confrontational. *United* takes its nod (sonically) from Kraftwerk's *Trans Europe Express* (1977) in its use of white noise as a percussion element, allowing the tracks to have a propulsive, steam-engine sense of momentum. In many ways, it's a study of minimalism, as repetitive themes from a synthesizer cast ominous and oblique harmonic patterns. The lyrics are upbeat and perhaps not reflective of what was to come on *The Second Annual Report* (1977). *Zyklon B Zombie* is a complete contrast: angry, distorted, and on the edge. It sets the mantra for forthcoming releases from the group—a world that moves between unpredictability and perverseness. Further to this, there is a flirtation with images and lyrics that provoke horrors of the past, presenting to the consumer a world full of horror with information without moral judgment. However, there is a 'blurred line between anguished awareness of horror and morbid fascination— bordering on identification with evil. Throbbing Gristle constantly teetered on the edge' (Reynolds 2005, 223–24). The group's use of electronics and the synthesizer is seminal on *20 Jazz Funk Greats* (1979), an album in which the sound and sonic palate of Throbbing Gristle really come to the fore.

## POSTCARDS FROM THE EDGE:
## *20 JAZZ FUNK GREATS* (1979)

In *Assimilate—A Critical History of Industrial Music*, the root of industrial music is considered, in its power to establish a strong sense of identity, of ideas, where bands often have a very strong visual aesthetic and that 'part of what makes industrial music's story compelling is the tension between all its theoretically rich ideology and the way that people have really engaged with it' (Reed 2013, 12). One only has to observe the absurdity and perhaps audacity of the cover of *20 Jazz Funk Greats*, which has multitudes of subversive meaning. Firstly, consider the image itself; in keeping with the theme of manipulating expectations, the members of the group posed as if out on a day trip, collecting samples from nature, innocent and free. Here, unknowing to fans unfamiliar with their previous works, the cover allows them to break with their own past. The cover, shot by Christopherson (Sleazy), is a skillful document in deception and kitch, deliberately altered to eject from previous ideas the group represents for both listener and, to a lesser degree, critic. Secondly, what's more menacing is the location: Beachy Head, East Sussex.

Known at the time as the most popular suicide point in Britain,[7] this statement of intent signifies the group's wish letter to its fans: never expect the same thing. One only has to draw the parallels between suicide and conformity to fully explore the cover in detail. What is deemed beautiful and peaceful is cast by the group into a flux of hidden meanings, and what is more sinister is their grinning faces.

Based on a more traditional lounge or exotica[8] music album cover format, it was a kilter of album covers at the time. Consider Joy Division's *Unknown Pleasures*, released in June 1979. Sleazy elaborates:

> At the time, there was no cultural knowledge or acceptance, no "lounge movement". Very few people knew who Martin Denny or Prezez Prado or any of those guys were, not like now where everything is pretty much available and known about. At the time the whole lounge aspect to it was something that was completely out of left field, and that aspect contributed to the weirdness of it. People in England at the time thought they knew who TG were—we were very noisy and dark and weird in the public's viewpoint, so twisting in this slightly sunny or lounge aspect was definitely a twist we hadn't made before. (Sleazy quoted in Reed 2013, 27)

It is performance art: the location, the smiles, the jumpers, and the Land Rover. The viewer and listener have quite a hard time putting themselves in the group's world in that the album cover is 'aesthetically soft but hermetically hard' (Daniel 2012, 29).

P-Orridge discussed further the subliminal ideas within the cover:

> Certainly Chris and/or Cosey were repulsed and attracted to Range Rovers at the time. The royal family had begun to use them. Maggie Thatcher's son endorsed them. What more fitting for the notorious "wreckers of civilization" than to appear to drive the same car as their arch cultural "enemies"? (Ibid., 31)

The cover was a mediated decision by the group in order to compound the listener's expectations, or perhaps they were just playing into the hands of popular music and its expected mechanics. Daniel again eloquently sums the cover as 'occupying a disappearing middle between boredom and disdain, the cover seems calculated to please no one' (Ibid., 35).

The sound of the group was informed by radical and nonconformism in music, much of which was informed by the West Coast of the United States when composers like Terry Reilly and La Monte Young were stretching musical minds by experimenting with time and repetition during the 1960s. Theirs was an attempt to raise the finger to contemporary classical music at the time, be it in sandals, mantras, and long beards. Nonetheless, it would be both East and West Coast American music that would prove to be most influential on the group. Bands like the Velvet Underground were certainly of influence with their references to death, sadomasochism, violence, and drug use. Not only that, but their focus and concentration was on making their image core, with sunglasses and leather pants being part of their uniform.

None of its members were trained musicians, and the bulk of their works are challenges to both popular musicmaking and the use of traditional rock instruments. Much of their recordings are composed of long improvisations being edited and treated as source material for recordings. One fundamental approach they incorporated into their anarchic philosophy to musicmaking was, like that of Throbbing Gristle, the 'non-musician.'

As discussed in chapter 4, Brian Eno was largely responsible for the popularisation of the 'non-musician' in Britain in the 1970s, and his knowledge of traditional music theory was limited. Lester Bangs probed Eno in 1979, enquiring:

LB: "Have you ever had any formal music or theory training at all?"

BE: "No."

LB: "Have you ever felt the pressure that you should get some?"

BE: "No, I haven't, really. I can't think of a time that I ever thought that, though I must have at one time. The only thing I wanted to find out, which I did find out, was what 'modal' meant, that was, I thought, a very interesting concept."[9]

What listeners will notice immediately when listening to *20 Jazz Funk Greats* is a total change in musical direction when considered against 1977's *2nd Annual Report*, which opens as dark, sullen, and unwelcoming. Not anymore, this one opens clean and crisp, with a drum machine startling the listener. With the end of the 1970s in sight, it was perhaps now time to experiment with a more digital sound and a sound palate that would condition many bands to a more formalised music.

The 'locked in' to the patterns and step sequences that instruments like the Roland TR-808 would provide, and indeed, industrial music of the 1980s, would see an array of acts using these machines to generate more dance-oriented industrial music, which included SPK and Skinny Puppy.

The album opener, '20 Jazz Funk Greats,' is hardly dystopian or industrial for that matter. It could be anyone, anything; all notions of linkage to both TG's sound to date and indeed the staples of industrial music's (dark, brooding) soundworld are gone. That is, until at thirty-six seconds in, the sounds of an atonal cornet and synthesizer make themselves known. The lyrics, or lack of, indicate abstract notions of what the listener is experiencing rather than a complete picture of what's to come. 'Jazz,' 'Tonite,' and 'Yeah' is not much indication of the album's contest, and it's a play on the album cover's concept.

Today, it is easy for us now to experience such diversions of an act's musical patch with the influence of streaming and instant access to the entire catalogue of recorded music, but it must have profoundly confused the listener of the late 1970s. While taking cue from the song's title, it does incorporate elements of these genres, improvisation from jazz, and perhaps repetition from funk music. Again, it is technology that is the driving force here. A key element in funk, the electric guitar, is here supplemented by two synthesizers playing solos, confusing and compounding musical norms, a postmodernist take on more traditional instruments. Further to this, perhaps the track's 'funk' elements are the interplays between the drum machine and the modular synthesizer.

The song fades out at two minutes and thirty seconds, throwing the listener into a position of confusion after perhaps providing (if only temporarily), a safe and nonoffensive place. Alas, we have just been duped, and what we have experienced is the group's successful attempt to wrongfoot audience expectations, something very much continued over from the COUM Transmissions' modus operandi and their 'we guarantee disappointment' mantra.

In a similar sense of immediacy, 'Beachy Head' follows, and once more, we are in familiar territory. It's stark and mysterious, almost like a calling to the shore, or head, as is the case. The guitar here seems to be stuck in space, flowing around our heads, and the field recordings buried underneath take us to that dark and lonely place for many, a last glimpse of the world around them. An important consideration here is the way in which the guitar is played; rather than being strummed, it incorporates an early version of an Ebow, in which a mechanised rubber wheel rubs against the all strings, thus producing large and continuous drones. If anything, this is what deep depression sounds like as it comes and goes, like a headache or a deep fog. The location here is evident; even the landscape of the cliff, prone to erosion, this sense of decay provokes a world full of unstable situations and perhaps, ideas. Place is crucial here, and the field recordings from Beach Head included in the composition are elemental, bringing us directly to that place through sound.

In any environment, our surroundings condition us, inform us how to operate, help us understand our habitat. It's hard to conceive of a space, so bound with rules and regulation, that is, in essence, transitory. Often, these spaces, which seem like part public spheres, are owned and managed either by government and private firms—each implying its own objectivity and onus of the control and regulation of space, in terms of security, atmosphere, ambience, and experience.

In *The Politics of Public Space*, Low and Smith (2006) define the difference between both public and private space, observing that:

> Public space is traditionally differentiated from private space in terms of the rules of access, the source and nature of control over entry to a space, individual and collective behaviour sanctioned in specific spaces and rules of use. (Low & Smith 2006, 1)

In discussing 'Beachy Head,' the representation of the place is key. Environmental psychology discusses the relationship of people within their physical setting. Studies in this area involve the evaluation of the interaction of people's behaviour and the perceptions toward spatial configurations as Sommer's (1974) *Tight Spaces: Hard Architecture and How to Humanise It*, discusses, in what he termed 'humanised places,' and Sommer argued that alienating environments produce subtle but psychological effects in all of us. He touches on this further in *Personal Space—The Behavioural Basis of Design* (1969), discussing how much an environment, or any environment for that matter, affects humans activities, writing:

> [Man] will adapt to hydrocarbons in the air, detergents in the water, crime in the streets, and crowded recreational areas. Good design be-comes a meaningless tautology if we consider that man will be reshaped to fit whatever environment he creates. The long-range question is not so much what sort of environment we want, but what sort of man we want. (Sommer 1969, 3)

Ultimately, what the group presents here in 'Beachy Head' is a process of how both location and environment can be provoked and transcended, as an everyday human experience, through sound. From something familiar to us, we are thrown into what can only be termed as 'psychotic disco' in 'Still Walking.' In this immersive sound mix, a comb filtered or flanged drum machine pulsates around us and provokes a harsh and metallic place. Battered by feedback and distorted guitar stabs, provided by Tutti, it's an alien place. This is further accentuated by P-Orridge's violin, which dominates the soundspace like a bully in the playground: pepped up, full of aggression, ready to fight. It is a suffocating mix, but what makes it even more chaotic is the call-and-response vocals, provided by P-Orridge and Tutti. Words like 'still walk-ing,' 'share of thee water,' 'in its element,' and 'like all of us' are panned across the mix. Their lack of clarity makes even more abstract this sense of hypnosis. P-Orridge's interest upcuts, a technique employed by the likes of William Burroughs, of whom he would later befriend, involved cutting up words and arranging them in different and nonsequential order, a ploy to perhaps confuse and overwhelm the listener.

Jazz improvisation features quite heavily on 'Tanith,' as a solo con-tribution from P-Orridge. Perhaps the most meandering composition on the album, this solo competition bass, distorted/processed violin, and vibraphone, with the addition of an auto-wah pedal, the sound world here is lost within itself. Its mood is something it shares with more contemporary jazz through abstraction and back-and-forth playing, the communication of instruments, and attempts to syntax of language.

Its duration unfortunately blocks us from further exploring the song's potential. Perhaps this is its very intention. In an attempt to bring you down from 'Still Walking,' the group uses improvisationally driven, directionally unexpected song form, and already we see its members stripping away much of the noise and nihilism of their past work to explore rhythm and melody more coherently.

'Convincing People' uses technology to deliver its message in a more clear and linear fashion, albeit a more sinister one. Here we have a soundworld that is disconcerting as P-Orridge discusses his notions on the title of the song. The delayed vocal, panned on the left and right of the mix, resembles very much an inner dialogue made public. As the song progresses, the presentation of the vocal becomes, at times, more childlike and psychotic. What surrounds the vocals is a distorted bass, and guitar figures as the monotonic, unchanging sequenced electronics drive on, without care as if ignoring the electronic elements floating around it. A study in alienation, what is interesting about this song is that the use of delay was its primary driver as P-Orridge, confirming that 'the delay on the voice that inspired the way the song was constructed.'[42] In an act of convincing people, such a nihilistic approach throws the listener into a state of paranoia, and again we hear the band's power to interchange, to complement themselves, to use extreme juxtapositions, all the while adding a clever sense of irony.

Dystopian and industrial drones reappear and bring us back to earlier works via 'Exotica.' Far from any relationship to the genre,[43] high frequencies ring backward and forward in an improvised place, while more melodic ones (and contrary to the background synthesised and phased instruments) produce a world of contradictions. If the vibraphones alone were to be put in isolation, they would indeed provoke sound worlds typical of exotica. However, the group successfully applies their own stance on what exoticas involves, as Daniel (2012) eloquently puts it, commenting that:

> Transposing the same formal strategies of group improvisation and collective feedback-looped mood summoning already employed on their harsher recordings, on "Exotica" TG reveal that all along their actual songs—qua songs—however texturally hard, are structurally soft. (Daniel 2012, 94)

What follows is perhaps the album's biggest statement of intent and most commercial track is 'Hot on the Heels of Love.' An intoxicating track that affixes the group's exotica obsession to a minimalist disco beat and Kraftwerk, that song would become a direct precursor to the entire genre of techno while also perhaps a homage to Giorgio Morroder and Donna Summers 1977 hit, 'I Feel Love.' In an act of sheer defiance of the listeners' expectations, beautiful arpeggiated sequences (one high on the right-hand mix, bass on the left) allow the proto-disco drums to have their own space while the vibraphones are meandering and wandering as per 'Exotica.'

The keyboard line is human-like, as if it's trying to speak a language unknown to us. Further commanding our attention is the snare that cracks and breaks any unwanted distractions. Carter's skill of programming really comes into focus here; it is reductionist and minimal, but this is part of its beauty. Yet what is most convincing are Tutti's vocals: 'I'm hot on the heels of love/waiting for help from above' are presented in a husky and sensual fashion, and it is very music, a sound document of a pornographic nature.

Technological leaps allowed the group to communicate with the contemporary pop music landscape; in the early 1980s, industrial bands, like Current 93 and SPK, were aligning themselves with pop. Again, brands like Korg and Roland allowed such acts to do this with much lower budgets. However, what is worth considering is that although a 'musician's tools might not entirely determine the music produced, they bear a strong influence on it' (Reed 2013, 130). Along with the 'Disco Sucks'[10] movement that occured in the United States and with Public Image Limited 'Death Disco' from the same year, the group attempts here to infiltrate the mainstream, to push their messages and subculture into the dancehalls and clubs. Ultimately, in line with other dance floor musical experience, the listener/ dander needs time to sit into the repetitive rhythm, to allow it to take command of their bodies. At four minutes and twenty-one seconds, while it is danceable and catchy, its short duration fails to allow us to get lost within it and maintains the kind of uncomfortable dissonance typical of an outfit lurking in the background of mainstream music.

As the compositional zigzag continues, 'Persuasion' throws us into a surrealistic realm where P-Orridge brings us into an uncomfortable unconscious realm of experience so completely that the world of dream and fantasy would be joined to the everyday rational world. The bass guitar essentially hammers us into a persuasion, unwillingly, while intermittent tape recordings try to provide a further glimpse of a narrative or a story that is essentially sordid and perverse. Such experiences must have resonated greatly with Tutti, who would have perhaps been in many persuasive situations as both a professional stripper and the star of a number of pornographic movies, as she comments:

> As the persuader, you only see the turn-on, you only see the positive
> side, because you're the one getting off on this. The other person isn't;
> they're just the vehicle for you to do that. In some ways, it's quite nice
> because you get a balance of me with my guitar. It's like a scream,
> shoutin, "No". When I look back on it now, that's exactly what I'm
> doing with the guitar. (Tutti 2017, 108)

'Persuasion' is both fantasy and control, and P-Orridge uncomfortably
draws a line between. Any indication of whether this 'Persuasion' is con-
sensual or not is unanswered, thus leaving the listener feeling unnerved and
perhaps now involved in something troubling.

In continuing the journey between emotional sonic arcs, 'Walkabout'
is the happiest moment on the record, and 'its placement both continuous
and exacerbates the sensation of music and emotional inconsistency in place
as the pendulum of *20 Jazz Funk Greats* swings in increasingly erratic directions' (Daniel 2012, 55). A nod to Nicholas Roeg's 1971 film *Walkabout*, the
track could be seen as a precursor to what would become Chris & Cosey,
formed after the demise of the group. As previously discussed, its sound
world is also a nod to Carter's siding with Krautrock or Kosmische Music and
showcases Carter's both compositional and technical skillset. Again an arpeggiated sequence bubbles throughout and feels like the most futuristic track
on the album. All this melody is perhaps, for some, a welcome relief from
the previous compositions. While Carter casts the direction of the album into
light, it is perhaps too much niceness too soon, as P-Orridge returns with a
chaotic 'What a Day.' If anything, it recalls the sound of the first Throbbing
Gristle releases, the industrial 'stamp of approval' of creating alienating sound
worlds. The instruments are aggressive; synths and guitars fight between
the mechanism of the electronics, much of which, primarily the rhythmic
elements, were made by sequencing Sleazy's found sounds and field
recordings on cassette. P-Orridge's vocals circle around the listener, and in
many ways, he changes character throughout, yet it's the repetition of these
words is perhaps the track's strongest element, as the listener creates their own
meaning by continuity exposure to this repetitive manifestation.

The album concludes with a broken-motor, grinding momentum
in the form of 'Six Six Sixties,' which, in many ways, sounds like a
live sound recording. Dark electronics overload the sound space that is
complemented with P-Orridge's wandering bass solo. The distortion used
acts as the album's epilogue; a last call into the wild, poised at the edge as
the lyrics (that dip into occultism) drive forward.

The album's reissue and liner notes sum up the acts approach, in that what they achieved with *20 Jazz Funk Greats* was both an intentional (and unintentional) exploration into the unknown, in that:

> The quality and content of this album should not be compared to conventional commercial live or studio recordings. The Throbbing Gristle repertoire consisted of intentional (and unintentional) tonalities, timbres including: tape hiss, phase errors, white noise, distortion, clicks, pops, extreme high and low frequencies and occasionally silence. Please bear in mind when listening to these recordings.[11]

*20 Jazz Funk Greats* pushes and pulls the group in and out of focus. In its flight between ugliness and beauty (through sound), and although it's a noncoherent musical directive, it's a very engaging listening experience. Its ever-shifting template, conceptual and process-oriented agenda, make it a milestone of dystopian, industrial music produced in Britain during the late 1970s.

In an exploration of such, *20 Jazz Funk Greats* does not seek truth or beauty; they simply dismantle it, using the synthesizer and electronics as a conduit to achieve this. Finally, in an apt and fitting analysis of the album, Daniel (2008) concludes a fitting summary of 'poised at the edge of the abyss, it's a record that can't make up its mind to jump or hang on' (Daniel 2008, 40).

## TECHNOLOGY

Throbbing Gristle's relationship with technology was a clear statement of intent as it acted as a platform to extend their interests in not only confrontation, but also in an attempt to challenge the listener. A clear example of this is alluded to by Fanny Tutti, commenting that 'Chris and Sleazy became very close, drawn together in frenzied enthusiasm for technology that could bring a new approach to and ways of making sound' (Tutti 2017, 242). The group did attempt to get endorsed by a number of electronics brands, as Tutti recalls, commenting:

> The Throbbing Gristle affair with Roland equipment started with Chris's synth and sequencers, then my Boss effects pedals, then we got a Roland Jazz Chorus combo amp. And thought what fun it would be to infiltrate the music-business practice of sponsorship deals. We

approached Roland, sending them a photo of us posing with all our Roland gear, They didn't bite. (Ibid., 244)

Indeed, these brands of electronics manufacturers helped shape the very sound of the group, as suggested by Tutti, in that:

> The rhythms Chris has done previously using tape loops were quite loose, allowing for more experimental, ambient tracks. We wanted to tighten things up. I loaned Chris £40 to part-exchange his Korg synth for a Roland Sequencer. He put rhythms together mostly in his flat, recording straight to tape using drum machines and synths, his new sequencer and tape samples. The Roland sequencer created the unrelenting rhythm that drove and anchored the Throbbing Gristle sound. '*Zkylon B Zombie*' took on a new life and we opened with it at our next gig. (Ibid., 226)

This rejection from a corporate electronics manufacturer was by no means a deterrent; it was in custom effects and homemade electronics that the group's sound, spurred on by Carter, would become further extended and came in the form of the 'Gristleizer.' The original Gristleizer unit was conceived and constructed by Carter but was based on an electronics DIY project designed by Roy Gwinn, which was published as the 'GEP' (Guitar Effects Pedal) in *Practical Electronics* magazine (July 1975). Roy Gwinn's project was also briefly sold in kit form (just the PCB and components) in the UK during the 1970s. Their musical and sonic legacy is reflected today with the numerous reincarnations of the Gristleizer, that included clones, in particular the ones developed by Endangered Audio in 2009.

Here, the sound worlds and sonic devices of the past are reformatted and reshaped for current generations to enjoy, and to perhaps create their own worlds of dystopian sonic futurism. The Gristleizer was remade in 2009 in conjunction with Industrial Records, TG, and Christian Virant (inventor of the widely popular FM3 Buddha Machine). This was a (more portable and reliable) reproduction of the original Gristleizer. It features thirteen TG loops that users can compose and make noise with. Carter is still very much at the forefront of maintaining TG's sonic legacy. Within the modular synthesizer world, in 2019, Carter, along with Roy Gwinn, developed a wide selection of eurorack[12] modules with Future Sounds Systems. Christopherson explained Carter's construction and musical experimentation in a 1987 interview with *Keyboard Magazine*, commenting:

> It was a box that [TG synthesist] Chris Carter made for me, to my design that basically switched on and off—through inputs on tape recorders—six

cassette machines, the output of each going to a different key. Many of the machines I used in TG were cassette machines that were stripped down and altered to play backward and forward and four tracks at once, the speed variable by flywheels. The very first sampling device there ever was, as far as I know, was manufactured by Mountain Hardware for Apple computers. It was designed to reproduce voice samples, and had a very limited selection of pitches. I was using that onstage in '79 or '80, which was before the first Fairlight was used commercially. So I've always had a soft spot for sampling.[13]

## CONCLUSION

Demers (2010) points toward one of Throbbing Gristle's key contributions to electronic music; the distortion of beauty, writing:

> The role of noise, repetition, stasis and distortion shifts to negative beauty, a pleasure that does not conform to Katian standards of balance and semblance but nonetheless aspires to the condition of beauty. The sublime and the beautiful are thus not so much opposites as they are different destinations along the same trajectory. (Demers 2010, 106–107)

The sound world the group created was produced by the misuse of both sythesthesizers and electronics. In this, they managed to achieve something unique, alongside the Punk movement, which was happening concurrently. By splitting both noise and music apart, their distortion of the traditional model of musicmaking would go on to spur numerous acts in Britain in the preceding decade. Indeed, the liberation of technology during the 1980s meant that the influence of TG would continue to inform in the guises of the split-off bands that the breakup would produced: Carter and Tutti's 'Chris and Cosey' and P-Orridge and Sleazy's 'Psychic TV' and 'Coil.' Along with Cabaret Voltaire, TG charted new territory and expanded borders of thought and the norms of musical performance that continue to influence the shape and sound of electronic music in Britain today. Their revolutionary attitudes and methods, rooted in both Dadaism and surrealism and transduced through means of confrontation and subversion, expressed Britain in the late 1970s like no other, its struggles and isolation.

Within the formation of the terms 'industrial music' as a genre, almost seems like accident and would come as much a surprise for the band, and this was come to bear on a November day in 1977, while visiting London's Virgin Records:

Saturday we went in to look around and see if it was on the shelves yet. We were looking around and it was not under *T*. We figured those fuckers hadn't put it out. We looked under I for industrial and there it was, written "industrial" and they spelled it wrong too. The next time we went in, there was Cabaret Voltaire there under *I*. They really swallowed it. They'd gone for it. Industrial music was now a genre. We were all, wow! we did it! We invented a genre of music![14]

On its release in 1979, *20 Jazz Funk Greats* polarised both the music press and its fan base. Rather than presenting a coherent collection of songs, what is evident is only fragments of ideas, always never resolved and 'neither ahead of its time nor entirely at home in its historical moment, its an album that never truly arrived' (Daniel 2012, 161). Yet it was such a powerful comment on modernity, a viewpoint of things that are broken, of social upheaval, viewed through the urban wastelands of 1970s Britain.

Berman's (2010) *All That Is Solid Melts into Air* considers the outcomes and realities of modernity, observing that:

> All these visions and revisions of modernity were active orientations towards history, attempts to connect the turbulent present with a past and a future, to help men and women all over the contemporary world to make themselves at home in this world. These initiatives all failed, but they sprang from a largeness of vision and imagination, and from an ardent desire to seize the day. It was an absence of these generous visions and initiatives that made the 1970s such a bleak decade. (Berman, 2010, 33)

Throbbing Gristle certainly 'seized the day' and spun the ideals and aesthetics of modernism to create, musically, something quite unique. *20 Jazz Funk Greats*' very failure to resolve could perhaps be the group's overarching and lasting influence, that of being flawed. The group was 'terminated' in 1981 and produced Psychic TV, Coil and Chris and Cosey, acts that would continue on their eternal musical journey of musical subversion.

### NOTES

1. See Savage (1991, 5).
2. See also https://www.theartstory.org/movement/viennese-actionism/ (accessed September 22, 2022).

3. COUM Transmissions also comprised more part-time members including Tim Poston, "Brook" Menzies, Haydn Robb, Les Maull, Ray Harvey, John Smith, Foxtrot Echo, Fizzy Paet, and John Gunni Busck.

4. This 'establishment' here was simply the older generation, so we are now witnessing the youth culture of the mid-1960s dramatically shifting in attitudes and values led by youth and was a worldwide phenomenon. The generations divided sharply by many issues including sexual freedom.

5. See also https://pdfslide.net/documents/tangerine-dream-sos-1.html (accessed July 10, 2022).

6. See also Kosmische Musik and its techno-social context, Alexander C Harden, *ISPM Journal* Vol 6, No 2 (2016). https://iaspmjournal.net/index.php /IASPM_Journal/article/view/784 (accessed July 10, 2022).

7. See also S. J. Surtees, "Suicide and accidental death at Beachy Head," *British Medical Journal* 284 (6312): 321–24, January 30, 1982, https://www.ncbi.nlm.nih.gov/pmc/articles/PMC1495868/ (accessed June 1, 2022).

8. Exotica was a form of music popular from the mid-1950s to the mid-1960s that evoked the unfamiliar, distant places and times, and used unconventional instruments to achieve this (xylophones, marimbas). See also Martin Denny's *The Enchanted Sea* (1951).

9. Lester Bangs, "Eno," Musician, Player, & Listener 21 (Nov. 1979), 40.

10. In 1979, the Detroit rock radio DJ Steve Dahl was so aggrieved that his beloved Stones and Zeppelin were being dropped from playlists in favour of the Village People, Donna Summer, and Chic, that he launched his "Disco sucks!" campaign. Dahl encouraged listeners to phone in their disco requests, which he would then destroy on air with explosive sound effects.

11. Liner notes, Remaster of 20 Jazz Funk Greats.

12. Eurorack is a modular synthesizer format originally specified in 1996 by Doepfer Musikelektronik. See also http://www.doepfer.de/home.htm (accessed September 1, 2022).

13. See also https://brainwashed.com/common/htdocs/publications/coil -1987-keyboard.php?site=coil08 (accessed March 10, 2022).

14. P-Orridge interview extracted from *Assimilate Magazine* https://www.tandfonline.com/doi/abs/10.1080/10486801.2011.645231 (accessed September 15, 2022).

# 6

# THE NORMAL

## The Car Crash Set

The English writer J.G. Ballard (1930–2009) wrote some of his most prolific work during the 1970s, works that painted images of bleak manmade landscapes and dystopian outlooks. Ballard also wrote about progress, albeit cautionary, and saw modernity as a landscape of bleak manmade sculptures. He was a primarily science fiction writer, and his early works were a direct response to his rejection of a particular type of 'England.'

Within this, Ballard attempted to deal with the psychological effects of technological, social, or environmental developments, and his obsession with mass media and emergent technologies would provide much influence on a generation of writers, artists, and musicians. This chapter discusses Daniel Miller's the Normal and the single 'Warm Leatherette' (1979), examining the influence of Ballard's *Crash* (1973) on Miller while also overviewing the synthesizers and electronics behind the work.

### INFLUENCES

Stout (1916), in *Art and the Automobile*, describes the ways in which power, body width, mass, comfort, and other automobile qualities can be suggested by proportions of the human body and that the automobile of the future would take every advantage of artistic knowledge to build up an appeal consistent with its mechanical performance, in that:

> Art is the science of eye appeal; the appearance-basis of attractiveness. If one builds into a commercial product an appeal to the eye, he establishes the first point of salesmanship, which is impression. (Stout 1916, 536–41)

The aesthetics with the mechanical were core to the Italian Futurist Movement (1909–1944), and in *The Founding and Manifesto of Futurism* (1909), F.T. Marinetti opens with a surrealist text, one full of 'speed, violence and dynamism' (Baxter 2009, 111). Here, the author is seated behind:

> the steering wheel, a guillotine blade that threatened my stomach, celebrates a new danger, which is also a new beauty: the beauty of speed. A racing car whose hood is adorned with great pipes, like serpents of explosive breath—a roaring car that seems to ride on grapeshot is more beautiful than the Victory of Samothrace. After the crash, the author is regenerated, rather than destroyed: When I came up—torn, filthy and stinking—from under the capsized car, I felt the white-hot iron of joy deliciously pass through my heart. (Marinetti 1909, 22)

This fusion of man and technology was at the core of the Futurist Movement. Through technology, Marinetti attempted to cross the boundaries of the self, subjectivity, reality, and the day-to-day experience. The Futurist Movement was largely concerned with what was referred to as 'dynamic aesthetics,' which involved glorifying modernity and breaking away from Italy's past. Marinetti saw the significance of the machine in that it could be eternal, always churning, driving toward both modernity and the future, albeit unknown. The industrialization in Italy (1897–1913) was a huge significance to the Futurist Movement, with many exploring the mechanisation of technology. The automobile, for Marinetti, explored futurism through a car crash. In the moment, he steps into modernism, a world where speed and technology explode (or crash) into his/her own progress. The rawness of this power, to engage within this new experience, Marinetti found, in the superior essence of progress, its major symbols, the car and:

> On we raced, hurling watchdogs against doorsteps, curling them under our burning tires like collars under a flatiron. Death, domesticated, met me at every turn, gracefully holding out a paw, or once in a while hunkering down, making velvety caressing eyes at me from every puddle. (Ibid., 186)

Another seminal text from the Italian Futurist Movement was Luigi Rossolo's *The Art of Noises* (1913). As Marinetti saw the car as a futurist conduit, Rossolo envisioned musicians to substitute, for the limited variety of timbres that the orchestra possesses, the infinite variety of timbres in noise and everyday life, reproduced via instruments more like machines.

The instruments that he and fellow futurist Ugo Piatti built, like the *Intonarumori*, were hand-cranked machines and exploited the Futurists' notions of noise, violence, and confrontation. Sixty years later, Ballard searched for new landscapes beyond what he observed on a daily basis, and these aspects of Britain were often marked by the 'overlapping, jostling vocabulary of science, technology, advertising: the new means of communication' (Paolozzi 2000, 204). Ballard discusses such notions in the introductory pages of *Crash* himself, commenting that:

> *Crash* is the first pornographic novel based on technology. In a sense, pornography is the most political form of fiction, dealing with how we use and exploit each other, in the most urgent and ruthless way. (Ballard 1995, 1)

The influence of mass media and technological change within society are key to Ballard's seminal 1973 book, *Crash*. This survey on the 'nightmare marriage between sex and technology' (Gasioreck 2005, 17) would become one of his most critically slated works. Gasioreck also points toward the 'libidinal potency of the automobile, the most obvious phantasmatic feature of this commodity, but also on its destructive power (literalised in the car-crash), [which] induces excitement and unleashes energy' (Ibid., 68). Invocations of machinery and psychosexual themes populate the book, as the 'crash' itself lies somewhere between the destructiveness of both human desires and technology. *Crash* is a 'cautionary book' (Ibid., 82) in that its 'depiction of a profound techno-cultural will to destruction marks it out as a modern morality tale' (Sobchak 1991, 18).

Vaughan, the book's central character, embodies this destruction and that of the 'body machine complex':

> I knew that Vaughan had retired finally into his own skull. In this over-lit realm ruled by violence and technology he was now driving forever at a hundred miles an hour along an empty motorway, past deserted filling stations on the edges of wide fields, waiting for a single oncoming car. In his mind Vaughan saw the whole world dying in a simultaneous automobile disaster, millions of vehicles hurled together in a terminal congress of spurting loins and engine coolant. (Ballard 1973, 16)

Gasiorek (2005) identified the 'crash' as having multiple resonances, in that:

> It excites to violence and exacerbates desire; couples the board with the machine; produces physical pain and proclaims human mortality;

transforms lives through the arbitrariness of the roadway collision; stages theatrical street-happenings for the voyeuristic gaze; and gives rise to an aesthetics of destruction characterised by unsettling techno-human sculptures. (Gasioreck 2005, 88)

Novelist Martin Amis was particularly crass in his review of *Crash,* referring to it as an 'indulgent exercise in vicious whimsy, 70,000 words of vicious nonsense' (Amis 1992, 92). Ballard scholar Jeannette Baxter, on the other hand, compared *Crash* to that of a work of 'avant-garde performance art' (Baxter 2009, 100). Baxter here was taking influences from Goldberg's 1979 *Performance Art: From Futurism to the Present,* in her observation on how performance art is 'often a permissive, open-ended medium with endless variables, moreover, the performance spectacle is a testing ground for dissonant experimentation and unorthodox expression' (Goldberg 1979, 9).

When Ballard was developing the book during the 1970s, performance art was gaining widespread notoriety, with, as previously discussed, the COUM Transmissions' 'Prostitution' exhibition in the Institute of Contemporary Art, London, in 1976, being of particular importance to the public awareness of performance art, helping it to assume the role of a new and dynamic platform for expression, one that often went beyond accepted notions of art.


## BACKGROUND(S)

Miller's The Normal fits into the lineage of the acts discussed thus far in that his approach was largely influenced by dystopian ideals, subversive art movements, industrial music, science fiction, and Punk aesthetics. Miller was making music as the dominance of white Anglo-American rock music was in decline. As Stubbs (2009) reflects, the impact of Punk on the establishment of popular music during the 1970s was extensive, observing that:

> Rock's lineage and hierarchy, its modernistic sense of progression based on hermetic and elitist notions of advanced musical proficiency had been brought crashing down. Moreover, punk was arguably the soundtrack to late capitalism in deep crisis. It was the noise of those deemed surplus to requirement—the people who made it were useless, as citizens and as musicians. From this, would spring punk's vitality. (Stubbs 2009, 84)

During the 1970s, capitalism was in crisis, and Punk both reflected and at the same time, deflected this, providing an escape from the 'gloom ahead amidst a certain grey, grim texture of everyday life in Britain, a country that seemed to have given up rationing only reluctantly' (Fisher 2015, 50). Rather than the synthesizer playing a secondary or support role, it was now at the front of the stage, pulsating and disfiguring rock music before its very eyes.

Technology was 'conditioning' the listener/audience, a technique writer William Burroughs was prone to implement as he used shock tactics and satire to pull the reader out of the drudgery of modern life. Technology refers to and reflects many sociotechnical systems and In the 1960s, media theorists attempted to classify their technologies. McLuhan (1964) first used the term *technophobe*, referring to it in that 'technology had reduced us to the sex organs of the machine world' (McLuhan 1967, 46). During this period, counterculture music and ideals were meditated, lyrically, often through the denouncement of corporate, bureaucratic, technological, and governmental control. Through processes such as automation, the concept that man is simply a control mechanism and that 'the machine' is now the ultimate tool for a tolerant society, was slowly becoming a reality.

For McLuhan, within this 'machine world' lay a futuristic, imagined hinterland, a land in which societal control and oppression are married. The machine—disciplined, nonverbal—acts as a demigod in a dystopian society, ready to serve man's every need, and McLuhan saw that, through mass media, advertising, and technology, a utopia was being presented to humans, and through it, the illusion of a perfect society. This, of course, is what was portrayed. The truth was, in fact, far more sinister.

Further to McLuhan and throughout the 1960s, academics, philosophers, and authors began to express criticism of the social, capitalistic, consumerist ethos and the supposed freedoms that come with it. Marcuse (1964) discusses ideas of 'freedom' in terms of the commoditization of technology, commenting:

> Technological rationality, which impoverishes all aspects of contemporary life, has developed the material bases of human freedom, but continues to serve the interests of suppression. There is logic of domination in technological progress under present conditions: not quantitative accumulation, but a qualitative leap is necessary to transform this apparatus of destruction into an apparatus of life. (Marcuse 1964, 11)

This 'quantitative leap' examines the very nature of technology that influences the demand for labour and capital. These matters, coupled with cuts in public spending and the struggles with the trade unions, helped shape the context of what electronic musicians and Ballard were exploring. Whereas Ballard sought refuge writing about dystopian worlds, musicians with synthesizers explored the realms of futurism to create a sound that referenced the landscape at that time—disconnected, harsh, and cold. This purports to the relationship between man and machine, a conversation long documented throughout both literary and musical outputs.

## THE CAR CRASH SET: *WARM LEATHERETTE* (1978)

One major thread that runs through Ballard's *Crash* is that of violence and, to some degree, varying levels of cruelty. Such themes are the basis of The Normal's single 'Warm Leatherette,' released on Miller's own Mute Records in November 1978. The B side of 'Warm Leatherette,' *T.V.O.D.*, was originally the lead single, and it was only in further reissues that 'Warm Leatherette' became the A side. Miller used the synthesizer and electronics to produce music without restriction. Miller, as a non-musician, often relied on accidental or unforeseen processes to help generate sounds, and this is often due to the performer's unfamiliarity of the instrument in question. Therein lies the power of technological change; invention and innovation allowed Miller to free himself from traditional pop music's sound reproduction mechanisms, that of learning how to play an instrument, traditionally. With this new and exotic futuristic tonality, Miller could extend lyrical detail, and within this, could produce more exotic and extreme thematic ideals.

The beginnings of the Normal came when Miller came off the road, along with Scottish musician Robert Rental, after supporting Stiff Little Fingers on a UK tour in 1979. Upon his return to his home, a number of cassette tapes awaited him. Miller, impressed with the quality and freshness of these demos, decided to do something, and soon Mute Records was born. The label would go on to define the sound of early 1980s Britain with a roster that included Depeche Mode, New Order, and Yazoo.

Founding an artist-led record label allowed Miller to bypass traditional music industry mechanics, ultimately allowing for great control of financial and creative content, again bearing claims of Punk's independent nature. Part of what makes a lead vocal so elemental in popular music is that it often commands our immediate attention, in that it contains the idea, mood, and subtext of a song, and it's here that the singer's personality appears. Both the lyrical content and the instrumentation of 'Warm Leatherette' make the song an exhilarating sonic ride in its very short duration of three minutes and twenty-five seconds. What is striking is Miller's use of the human voice, and its presentation contains stimulating physical connotations and associated images. Images of contorted flesh and metal paint the song's lyrical structure, one that portrays the scenarios of a car crash. Through listening, we are propelled into this, in real time becoming unwilling passengers.

Vocally, its delivery is static, with repetition playing a key role with the words 'Warm Leatherette' appearing again and again, mantra-like, as if Miller is programming the words into our brains. The images generated are so startling that as listeners, we are barraged, from start to finish, with images of death, sensuality, and violence. Similarly, the abrasive nature of music throws us back and forth, in flux. We are the victims in some way, being manipulated through aural stimulation. It draws on many thematic ideas within both Ballard's and Miller's depiction of pain for pleasure. Miller, like Ballard, takes the central theme of the sexualisation of pain and death as a lyrical basis, and ultimately, like the central themes in *Crash*, its characters strive toward a fusion with their machines in a death pact.

Instrumentally, the song is constant, nonstop, and at times, it's hard to catch your breath—one blink, and you might miss a thought central to its remit. Minimalist concepts are key to the work, although only two chords are used throughout. Much like the sonic landscape of a car crash, the instrument's tonalities are harsh and crass; the kick drum draws on images of a car's wheel passing over road markings at speed, acting as a time maker and providing a sense of duration and metre. The snare drum, on the other hand, cracks back and forward like a whip, drawing us closer to the subject matter of the song itself. Melodically, a monophonic synthesizer wails back and forth, almost like an alarm, provoking a sense of imminent danger. Further to this, a synthesised bass helps keep a constant presence, and only temporarily are we relieved of the second, higher oscillating tone that commands our attention further.

## TECHNOLOGY

In 1977, the French composer Pierre Boulez published an article entitled 'Technology and the Composer,'[1] and within this, he questioned the relationship between the composer, the producer, and the instruments they employ. Although based on the composition of a more academically themed electronic music, its concepts parallel similar performance aesthetics of 'Warm Leatherette.' Boulez discussed the dialectical relationship between both musical material and ideas and proposed that musical invention must bring about the creation of the musical material it needs; by its efforts, it will provide the necessary impulse for technology to respond functionally to its desires and imagination, and this process will need to be 'flexible enough to avoid extreme rigidity and impoverishment of an excessive determinism and to encompass the accidental or unforeseen' (Boulez 1977, 23).

Boulez highlighted that both the non-musician and the synthesiser rely on such 'accidental or unforeseen' processes to help generate sounds that are generated by chance, often due to the performer's unfamiliarity of the instrument in question, as discussed previously.

Such invention, innovation, and technology allowed Miller to free himself from traditional pop music's sound-reproduction mechanisms. With regard to early electronic music devices from brands such as Korg and Roland, the sheer abrasiveness of the instrument's tonality was part of its selling point. Economic reasons played a significant role in how 'Warm Leatherette' actually sounded. This, coupled with a lack of informal playing, led to the distinctive sound of the Normal and others. Part of a synthesizer's power, in regard to the Normal, is this: When predetermined conceptual ideas are left out of the equation, real-time reaction often replaces interaction. This shift allowed Miller to create real-time responses to the music generated, as, although rigid in the structure, it could at any moment become flexible and versatile through improvisation with the machines. Part of the reward in using analogue technology is its levels of instability and perhaps unreliability in that artists using such electronic instruments often are learning about their operation during the compositional process. This can, at times, produce unexpected results, often leading to new and innovative effects, ideas, and processes that might not have appeared whilst using traditional instruments. Within this learning curve, the removal of the ego is born, and gone, for a time, is popular music's ethos of traditionally nurturing an individual's instrumental dexterity. This detachment or disconnection from established norms with popular music made the sound of the Normal so distinctive.

Part of a synthesizer's power, in regard to the Normal, was that when predetermined conceptual ideas were left out of the equation, reaction often replaced interaction, as Miller observes:

> The role of electronic music is no longer so distinct; the lines are completely blurred when everyone is recording using computers, and can apply however many effects. My personal position in defining electronic

music is simply to state everything has to start with a sine wave. (Miller, quoted in Collins et al. 2003, 292)

Technology allowed Miller to create real-time responses to the music generated, as, although rigid in the structure, it could at any moment become flexible and versatile through improvisation with the machines. Part of the reward in using analogue technology is its levels of instability and unreliability in that using such electronic instruments often involves learning about their operation during the compositional process. This can, at times, produce unexpected results, often leading to new and innovative effects, ideas and processes that may not have appeared whilst using traditional instruments.

Economic reasons played a significant role in how the Normal sounded, as Miller used a Korg 700s synthesizer, far cheaper than Moog's equivalent, and this, coupled with a lack of informal playing, led to the distinctive sound of the Normal. The 700s, a monophonic analogue synthesizer used later by acts such as the Cure and the Human League, was a very primitive machine, with no performance controls like pitch or modulation. It was the perfect machine for 'Warm Leatherette,' controlled and restricted, and in such, the beauty of the song is its minimalist approach, encapsulating Miller within the limitations of the instrument itself.


## CONCLUSION

Popular music by its very nature is conservative, and it was through this new relationship with technology that Miller and others could now free themselves of traditional sounds and their reproduction. This alteration and change within this relationship involved a crucial element, the microchip—the conduit that made it all possible. The sheer abrasiveness of the instrument's quality is part of its selling point. The beauty of these electronic devices is this: When determined conceptual ideas are left out of the equation, reaction replaces interaction. This dialogue allowed Miller to create real-time responses to the music that, although rigid in the structure, could at any moment become flexible and versatile through the use of the musical equipment employed.

Part of the reward (for some) in using synthesisers is their level of instability. This can often produce unexpected results, leading to new and innovative effects, ideas, and processes that might not have appeared whilst using a guitar or drum kit. Levels of instability meant the machine could go belly-up at any minute.

This instability also reflects the times in which 'Warm Leatherette' was created. By working directly with sound, Miller was able to bypass music theory and notation. In the midst of Punk rock, the song reflects music and society, providing a soundtrack to the feelings of change and decay. Within this, the removal of the ego is born, and gone is rock music's ethos of nurturing individual instrumental dexterity.

For Miller, the use of the synthesizer allowed for these levels of interaction to remain in human hands, and perhaps this is central to why its sound was so convincing as a futuristic sonic experience in 1978. Ballard's 'Crash' and Miller's 'Warm Leatherette' embody similar creative and aesthetic ambitions. Through the presentation of a radical document in both text and sound, they attempted to present to late-1970s Britain the sense of the unknown and, socially and culturally, the unstable.

## NOTE

1. *Times Literary Supplement* (London), May 6, 1977. See also https://www.jstor .org/stable/1573509#metadata_info_tab_contents (accessed May 5, 2022).

# 7

## FAD GADGET

## Mechanised Curiosity

The tools for making electronic music are an interface to 'ghosts of technoscientific projects past,'[1] and as Cascone (2011) observes, one of technology's roles is to hide its failures, in that:

> Failure has become an important prominent aesthetic in many of the arts in the late 20th century, reminding us that our control of technology is an illusion, and revealing digital tools to be only as perfect, precise and efficient as the humans who build them.[2]

Attali (1977) suggests that every code of music is 'rooted in the ideologies and technologies of its age, and at the same time produces them,'[3] commenting:

> Economically, the new technology creates a supply of a product, but it must also create a demand for an object that outlasts its use. (Attali 1977, 100)

Attali saw that music, as a cultural form, was intimately tied up in the mode of production in any given society and indeed, its cultural stages in its history, and it is suggested here that it is up to the musicians to question the validity of a technology and its contribution.

When we define an artist's work within a category, it is placed within a genre of ease of access classification. Yet so many factors influence this process—social relations, class, economics—and through this, 'popular music illuminates place, either directly through lyrics and visuals, metaphorically through heightened perceptions, through sounds that are seen as symbolic of place and in performances that create spaces of sentiment' (Connell et al., 88). We must consider the background of these musical communities, some of which were stuck between the rhetoric of tradition and modernity, the past and the future, the local and the global, questioning the culture and politics such musical beginnings caused. Such topics are currently being explored via the reissuing (and often repackaging) of records made in the past.

The life and times of Francis John Tovey (1956–2002) is often overlooked with the histories of both early new wave and industrial music, and much of his back catalogue is now being reissued. Taking more of a direction from Einstürzende Neubauten, across his discography lies a solid collection of works that employ a multitude of approaches and genres, from pop to noise and everything in between.

Of all the acts documented in this book, his work was perhaps overwhelmingly more direct in terms of social commentary, almost always delivered in a monotone and deadpan voice. In what can be seen as verified and not entirely consistent, within his discography he delivered paintings washed with a dark dystopia, and with this sentiment in mind, this chapter explores Tovey's album *Fireside Favourites* (1980).

Tovey's work has been cited as a major influence on upcoming acts during the early 1980s, like Depeche Mode and Orchestral Movements in the Dark. It would be the Normal's and Mute Records' Daniel Miller who would prove key to Tovey's early career, as Miller recalls: 'Fad Gadget was the first one (demo) I liked enough to put out. Before I knew it, I was running a record company—working from home with no staff or anything like that, but a record label nonetheless' (Miller, quoted in Reynolds 2005, 99).

## INFLUENCES

Extending the idea of live performance was key to Tovey, in particular with regard to 'shock,' and this would play an important role in the early part of his career. In particular, acts like Throbbing Gristle use this process most successfully, perhaps more as COUM Transmissions. For many of the groups documented in this group, as the 'hippie' movement fizzled out, many sought and found influence in the past: the Italian Futurists, Dada to Situationist Movements. From this, both performative and aesthetical ideals were formed, and a form of philosophical propaganda was born, which in many ways established part of their legacies and influence on what was to come later in the 1980s with acts like Nitzer Ebb and Skinny Puppy.

Reed (2013) presents the writings of Antonin Artaud (1896–1948), playwright, actor, essayist, and key player in the Surrealist Movement in Paris from 1924 to 1926, as an interesting, cross-pollinating framework for the works and practices of industrial music, in that 'Artaud empowers an aesthetic means of shock, calls on the grotesquery of the gothic, demands the bodily, and implements this all in a political framework' (Reed 2013, 169).

Reed offers here a connection to industrial music and the avant garde, and in particular toward Artaud's 1932 manifesto that 'serves as a prescient blueprint for industrial performance, particularly in its celebration of the abject and its distaste for camp' (Ibid., 168).

The Surrealist Movement was deeply influenced by the events of World War I, and many of its members believed the exploration of the unconscious mind was the way forward for the arts. Political differences led to his expulsion from the group by its leader, Andre Breton, and he went on to found Theatre Alfred Jarry with Roger Vitrac and Robert Aron. Artaud's *The Theatre and Cruelty* (1932) was an intense drama movement that involved what could be considered a multimedia event, with props, lighting, and more importantly, the element of shock. Thematically, it involved themes of introspection, drug use, and mental health, to which Artaud was later diagnosed with schizophrenia and was unable to adapt to life. He could not relate to others, and he was not even certain of his own identity in that 'Artaud was in essence constructing an entire metaphysical system around his sickness, or, if you will, entering the realm of the mystic via his own disease. The focal point of his universe was himself and every-thing radiated from him outward' (Knapp 1980, 226). Although he spent the last remaining years in psychiatric clinics, his influence on the European avant garde was immense, particularly on writing from Samuel Beckett, philosophers Gilles Deleuze and Felix Guattari, and American poet Allen Ginsberg, whose poem 'Howl' (1954) would go on to inspire the beat generation of writers.

Reed (2013) continues, in that 'to lovers of surrealism, to the dedicat-edly paranoid, and to many self-declared freethinkers, Artaud is a symbolic figure not merely for his writing and theatre but for what they perceive to be a self-sacrificing commitment to the pan-revolutionary' (Reed 2013, 171).

The work of Tovey and Fad Gadget moves across the surrealist sphere, in particular. Tovey used the avant garde for inspiration with both con-frontational and physical live performances that established him, like many others of the time, as expressly nonconformist. His identity was born in this fashion, and his creation of a chaotic and noisy method was to challenge the aesthetics of the establishment (be it the government or perhaps the music industry as a whole). Tovey used his body as a platform for expression, and akin to Artaud, Tovey used his identity as a spectacle. For many in the current 'scene' of acts, with the concurrent movement of Punk occurring culturally at the same time, attitude and persona was (and perhaps still is) as valuable as the musical output of an act or group. This type of status and subversion has now been sadly replaced by social media, and it can perhaps no longer create this sense of rawness and newness, the esoteric and misfit.

## BACKGROUND(S)

Cox and Warner (2004) point out that, over the past half century, an emerging audio culture appeared as an 'explosion of interest in auditory history and anthropology led by social scientists who have turned their attention to sound as a marker of temporal and cultural difference.'[4] Further to this, the creative possibilities of sound recording and repro-duction challenged the score-governed field of European art music. This explosion in sound and its production was viewed by French philosopher Jacques Attali, akin to both economics and politics, as a system of organ-isation through dissonance, and that harnessing the power of music was a reflection of society in that:

> With music is born power and its opposite: subversion. In noise can be read the codes of life, the relations among men. Clamour, Melody, Dissonance, Harmony; when it is fashioned by man with specific tools, when it invades man's time, when it becomes sound, noise is the source of purpose and power, of the dream—Music. It is at the heart of progressive rationalisation of aesthetics, and it is a refuge for residual irrationality; it is a means of power and a form of entertain-ment. (Attali, 1977, 6)

Attali saw the power of the organisation of sound, its control, and more importantly, the sense of power it could provide. Even at an early stage, Tovey was keen to explore this form of power, sound recording, and like the many acts covered in the book, the tape machine and/or tape recorder was the technology of choice.

It was during his first experiments with tape machines that the idea of noise became of interest to Tovey, and this, coupled with the more subversive elements of his music, became elemental in his early work. After a period in Leeds Polytechnic studying visual arts, Tovey's first experiments with sound and music were very low-key, as 'there was very little space the house I was living in in London and the only place I could buy a studio was in my cupboard' (Tovey 1984, 29). These early experiments soon evolved into solid tracks, and some time spent recording in London's RMS studios produced the single 'Back to Nature.' Much of this recording was both produced and supervised by the Normal's Daniel Miller, who signed Tovey to Mute Records and released the single in October 1979. He was inspired to make music and to start Mute by the Punk movement, in that:

> Punk had this incredible energy, but musically it became very conser-vitaive very quickly. It sounded like sped-up pub rock, and it was very exciting for a moment, not just musically, but also just because it was so disruptive. So I went back to film editing to make some money. I bought a cheap second-hand synth and a second-hand tape recorder and started playing around at home. I had no idea what I would be able to do. I just wanted to try it. And then I started enjoying it. (Tovey, quoted in Jones 2020, 119)

Punk became, at this stage, an export and a wider repose of England's wider social and cultural changes. York (2020) considered it as such in that 'you could not just write it off as just tourism; you can't just say it isn't relevant to a discussion of design futures. Because that stuff, the class stuff, the archaic stuff, the great dressing-up box of the past, is massively important in selling things and ideas from Britain' (York, 2020, 95).

'Back to Nature' shares the same sound world as the Human League's June 1978 single, 'Being Boiled,' in its cold and dystopian craftsmanship. Another single, 'Ricky's Hand,' followed swiftly in March 1980, and it again featured Miller heavily, writing, playing, and producing. Recorded in London's Blackwing Studios, it features more elaborate recording devices; notably Miller's Arp 2600 and Roland SH-2 synthesizer, along with a Black & Decker V.8 Double Speed Electric Drill.[5] Having now established his sound, along with the use of found objects and electronics, Tovey was invited by Miller to produce his debut LP, *Fireside Favourites* (1980). Although it did not reach the commercial charts, it would go on to set the template for both industrial and Post-Punk records of the early 1980s, in particular in continental Europe with the Anglo-French group, Hard Corps, and Germany's Belfegore. More so, it would be Depeche Mode that would cross over and populate the industrial sound into the charts, and in the early 1980s this 'popularity gave mass audiences a reference point for industrial music's clear influence, even if they'd never heard the genre's name' (Reed 2013, 232).

## PEDESTRIAN WAIT: *FIRESIDE FAVOURITES* (1980)

Signal processing has the power to take a simple sound like a sine wave and transform it into something futuristic, unconnected from traditional instruments. As modes of digital synthesis dominated throughout the 1980s, in particular with the advent of MIDI in 1983, the role of the synthesizer changed; it was no longer about obscuring the sound signal; it was more so reliant on the 'imitation' of more traditional instruments. The English electronic musician Scanner (Robin Rimbaud) discussed such imitations, arguing that:

> Synthetic production presents cultural artifice, the sign, the map of recognition, as a substitution for the real, an alternative vernacular, "as signs of the real for the real itself: as Baudrillard argued. The erasure of historical reference points within this imagined synthetic universe has developed into simulacrum, which differentiates itself from representation in the sense that a simulacrum marks the absence, not the existence, of the objects it's supposed to signify." (Rimbaud, cited in Demers 2008, 46)

Rimbaud eloquently references Baudrillard's (1981) *Simulacra and Simulation*, a philosophical text that examines and explores postmodernity and the relationships between culture and media. The role of the production of the 'synthetic' via the synthesizer probes cultural production and its expenditure and claims that much of society has been replaced by signs and symbols.

Within this translation, much of the human experience was now a simulation version of reality in that 'simulation is no longer that of a territory, a referential being or a substance. It is the generation by models of a real without origin or reality: a hyperreal' (Baudrillard 1988, 166). Baudrillard's work touches on both mass media and its reproduction, and it is referenced here as Tovey's *Fireside Favourites* was released at the dawn of the 1980s, a new decade in which both culture and materialism would shift quite significantly, particularly in London, where a new breed of social class was developing, as Jones (2020) points out, in that:

> Pigeonholing then became something of a 'thing', as yuppies (Young Urban Professionals) were heralded as the unacceptable face of pro-

fessional success; few synthesised concepts of class and status have acquired so much amoral resonance so quickly. They were followed in quick succession by guppies (gay urban professionals), dinkies (double income, no kids), donkeys (double income, no kids), dockneys (east Dockland London yuppies), puppies (Porsche-owning urban professionals). (Jones 2020, 242)

As parts of London was transitioning from brick and mortar to glass and modernist façades, Tovey assembled a team of another form of 'yuppies': engineers and producers at Blackwings Studios in the summer of 1980, a team that included the Normal's Daniel Miller (synthesizer and electronic percussion), Eric Radcliff (guitar), John Fryer (percussion), and Phil Wauquaire (bass).

The album opens with 'Pedestrian,' and its lyrical theme parallels with Miller's, that of the automobile and the dominance of roads and its associated pollution. Its delivery is authoritative, and the track is upbeat, which in many ways sets the album up in the Post-Punk genre. Its jagged and angular guitar parts, more than likely processed by Miller's Arp 2600, Tovey supplements and support lyrics of warning:

Every road leads to another,
Juggernaut Noise and Petrol Fumes.

Even though Tovey here points toward his dislike of machinery, along with these found objects, drills and electric shavers became core to the album's overall sound world. Elsewhere, Tovey uses more abrasive and more shock value:

Don't breathe the air,
It's full of lead,
Baby's sick,
Baby's dead.

Tovey used an interesting vocal technique by also punctuating the ending of each bridge by singing the ending lyric with a shout, which is further processed by reverberation.

The song ends with a wash of white noise and distortion that bleeds into the next track, and with 'State of the Nation.' Here Tovey delivers lyrics with a deadpan, monotonous leaning. Drums and bass lead with a dominant swing. However, the synthesizers provide much of the musical components; further to this, the background noise and electronics wash across much of the track, crescendoing at the end to a chaotic sound space that is harsh and abrasive. It can only be assumed here that much of this has been created by the sound of drills, as mentioned in the LP's liner notes, and the addition of the wash of noise supports the song's pessimistic overview with Tovey singing, 'Life begins when you're ready to face it.'

The song's title also refers somewhat to the decline and eroding of the status of the British empire, as Tomlinson (2013) indicates that 'the problems of the mid-1970s were not short term but the culmination of a long-term decline, deeply embedded in British society and in its political economy' (Tomlinson, quoted in Black, Lawrence, Pemberton, Hugh, & Thane, Pat [eds.] 2013, 55). Commenting on consumerism as at the dawn of a new decade, both banks and government were pursuing a policy of pushing affluence as 'domestication, central heating, freezers and home telephones became more common in British homes' (Black & Pemberton 2013, 16). Tovey narrates:

Collecting things don't need
In a room I never use.

As the song peters out, we are left with a stagnant feeling, yet with a sense of questioning the very nature of being. 'Salt Lake City Sunday' jumps into action, pulling the listener out of a dystopian slumber.

At two minutes and twelve seconds, it's the album's shortest track that combines proto techno, upbeat, and marching band music (that is supported by Nick Cash's drumroll) to create a unique and diverse addition at such an earthly stage of the album. Lyrically, the Church of the Latter-Day Saints (LDS) are the target here, and Tovey's presents a wiry commentary: 'They want you to repent/they want your ten percent.' Although not seemingly religious, Tovey uses this lyrical content to further underpin his distaste for the organisation of loft spiritual thoughts, including those of the LDS, which included the 'baptism of the dead,' in which individuals who had died without accepting the church's gospel and no longer possessed the physical body for baptism were represented by living proxies.[6] A distorted and improvised synthesizer solo, along with a dynamically changing drumroll, takes the track to an anxious climax, in which Tovey gives his ultimatum to perhaps the LDS: 'I slam the door in your face.' 'Cotius Interruptus' begins with a drum motif that would not be out of place on a disco LP. This soon alters, and a repetitive synthesised theme begins and continues throughout the track. Thematically, another concept is tackled: society and that of empty relationships. Its sound world is full of a deviant coldness, a depraved sexuality, as Tovey grunts his way through, commenting;

The boys sleep with girls
The boys sleep with boys
Never find that high
Never acting coy.

In a 1981 interview, Tovey goes into further detail about the track's theme:

> *Coitus Interruptus* is about...see, every disco record I've ever heard seems
> to be about having sex, the girl songs about sex are about being in love,
> and the man sex songs are about getting a woman and having your way
> and all this. So I thought I'd write a song that was a disco song and that
> was really sexual, thumping—I can imagine a lot of people dancing in
> discos to it—but which is about not being able to have sex properly—
> trying it, but it goes wrong—because all songs seem to be about having
> sex. It's like what Boyd was saying the other day, if you write a song
> about hate, hating somebody, people will think, "Oh, it's really odd,
> it's strange," but nobody thinks it's strange writing songs about loving
> somebody. Nearly every song in the chart is about love, so why should
> it be strange writing something about hate? There are always songs
> about sex, so I thought I'd write about sex going wrong, because sex is
> not always great.[7]

The vocal grunts throughout become increasingly guttural, a struggle from
within, faced with the bleak and modernist point of view of intimacy. The
electronically processed guitar adds a significant weight to the clustered
sounds, and Tovey has a call-and-response interaction with this as the song
ends with the vocals pulsating parts of the finishing line. Sex and sexuality
have been extensively explored by other acts documented in this book,
most notably Throbbing Gristle, yet here Tovey explores similar territories;
desire and death are wrapped in a dark and dangerous musical atmosphere.

'Fireside Favourite' was released as the album's first single by Mute in
June 1980, and as the album's title track, it is perhaps the most quirky contribution to the album. Set amidst a nuclear meltdown, this proto love story
and its lyrical contents are satirical and cynical, and along with the slow and
swinglike waltz timing, the drum machine (unknown model) provides the
main drive for the track. Within this, Tovey is in his own cabaret show,
detailing circumstances of a apocalyptic love:

There's a mushroom cloud up in the sky,
Your hair is falling out and your teeth are gone,
Your legs are still together,
But it won't be long.

The themes of human interaction appear again, but here it's the idea of conquest and its loss or unattainability in the modern world. Musically, it's repetitive, marching along at a midtempo pace, and it sounds very much like early Human League.

'Newsreel' accelerates the intensity of the album upward with perhaps the most Post-Punk addition so far. The drum machine and live drums add significant motion to the track, along with the reverberated percussion, and again it's hard to distinguish if we are hearing electronics or processed guitars. Here Tovey expresses his view on the media, his disdain for the media of television that focuses more on sensationalism than cold, hard news. Tovey used his nervous energy here to perhaps be as provoking as the tabloids in the track's open lyrics with: 'point the camera at the baby, shoot the mother, giving birth.' As per 'Pedestrian' and 'State of the Nation,' 'Newsreel' is social commentary, about slugging through modern life. Again we must consider the political climate of the time, and during the period of 1977–1980, the press was largely at fault for propagating levels of public concern or what led to the phenomenon of 'moral panic,' in that:

> Societies appear to be subject, every now and then, to periods of moral panic. A condition, episode, person or groups of persons emerges to become defined as a threat to societal values and interests; its nature is presented in a stylised and stereotypical fashion by the mass media; the moral barricades are manned by editors, bishops, politicians and other right-thinking people; socially accredited experts pronounce and their diagnoses and solutions; ways of coping are evolved or (more often) resorted to: the condition then disappears, submerges or deteriorates and becomes more visible. Sometimes the object of the panic is quiet novel and at other times it is something which has been in existence long enough, but suddenly appears in the limelight. (Cohen, quoted in Osgerby 2014, 188)

This 'limelight' was often perpetuated by the media and tabloids that contributed to the rise and oscillation of social unrest, often misreading and misinterpreting the events of the world. Further to this, Tovey is, thematically, battling against an authoritarian form of a political system, as some of the track's titles suggest. As the 1980s began, the media's response to society's woes only increased from hooliganism to how the government dealt with the AIDS crisis during the early 1980s.

'Incestiside' follows, and many of the tracks that appear on the album are proto or early sketches of future musical genres, in this case electro-punk. Tovey's vocals are heavily distorted by both ring modulation and phase effects. Its repetitive melodic theme haunts the sound space as Tovey now takes lyrical content from the point of view of a fly, as Tovey repeats: 'smashing my face against the windowpane.' This claustrophobic and nervous energy is further supported by a synthesised arpeggiated melody, which, along with other instruments (including what sounds like the drill), creates a chaotic and distorted atmosphere. Released as a highly contrasted B side to the album's only single, 'Fireside Favourite,' in June 1980 and at only three minutes and ten seconds long, it is perhaps the album's oddest contribution.

Feelings of claustrophobia and nervousness continue into 'The Box.' Again, Tovey takes on another persona, possibly that of a film director, in which we become privy to a number of death scenes. The track first appeared as the B side of the single to 'Back to Nature,' released in October 1979. As Tovey exclaims, 'Let me out,' it's easy to assume that 'the box' is indeed a metaphorical one, or perhaps not; it could indeed be a burial of sorts. Musically, it builds gradually from a more minimal sound stage to, like many of the tracks so far, a chaotic, nervous building to a climatic and sudden stop, like slamming the brakes on an uncontrollable car.

The album concludes with the cinematic soundscape of 'Arch of the Aorta.' One can hear elements of David Bowie's *Low* (1977), and it can only be assumed that Gary Numan was influenced by this epic-sounding contribution. The musical elements are surrounded by a voiceover and a conversation between a nurse and a doctor that is somewhat distorted at times. At six minutes, twenty-one seconds, the layered guitars are heard, and due to their lack of lyrical sound, it perhaps gives us time to reflect on the album as a whole. It's evident to hear that this closing track in many ways solidifies Tovey's contribution, as this sound would become synonymous with the sound of industrial music in the 1990s, in particular with acts like Nine Inch Nails. Ultimately, Tovey was not particularly satisfied with the album, commenting:

> I think I did the best I could do in that situation at the time, but I'm never satisfied with anything I do. I can always see how I can improve it. So I'm never totally satisfied with something, which I think is good in a way, because if I thought the album was good and something very special, then there wouldn't be any point in carrying on. The reason why I carry on is to improve on what I have already done. That's why I tried to redo *The Box*. I'm not sure if it worked. A lot of people said they don't think it's as good as the original. But what I tried to do with that was the song was about claustrophobia, about being trapped in something, and I wanted to try and give it more of a claustrophobic

feeling. I don't know if I achieved that or not. I actually recorded the vocals inside a box, I sang in a box so that it would sound like I was closed in, but you can't really hear that.[8]

Aside from Tovey's more downbeat analysis of *Fireside Favourites*, the album was seminal in shaping the sound of both experimental and industrial bands of the 1980s, including SPK, Front 242, and Nitzer Ebb. Although forgotten and ignored by both the music industry and his peers on release, much of Tovey's legacy lies in what genres the sound of the album would go on to influence: synthpop, EBM, techno, and more so, acts like Depeche Mode, that would go on to borrow heavily from Tovey, both musically and stylistically. In a turn of events, Tovey's biggest live shows would be toward the end of his life, supporting Depeche Mode on their Exciter Tour in 2001. Sadly, Tovey died in April 2002 at forty-five due to a lifelong heart defect, just as a whole new generation and audience were beginning to appreciate his brand of subversive and dystopian music.

## TECHNOLOGY

Our relationship with technology conditions us, or as Heidegger wrote, 'the will to mastery becomes all the more urgent the more technology threatens to slip from human control.'[9] The removal of technologies' intended functionality, and the creative abuse of it, offers the opportunity to exploit a sounding object by any means necessary in order to access its potential sonic palette.

Virilio (2003) highlights the loss of physicality within current electronic musicmaking, commenting that:

> The demise of the relative and analogue character of photographic shots and sound samples in favour of the absolute, digital character of the computer, following the computer, following the synthesizer, is thus also the loss of the poetics of the ephemeral. For one brief moment Impressionism—in painting and in music—was able to retrieve the flavour of the ephemeral before the nihilism of contemporary technology wiped it out once and for all. (Virilio 2003, 48)

One cannot help but wonder about the possibilities (or lack thereof) of future formats that may appear. A universal and accepted classification of Fad Gadgets' music is not possible due to the proliferation of dialects and techniques Tovey used in making the music he made within the genre. In attempting to do so, and with a very limited range of literary sources available, Fad Gadgets' discography is very much part of the dystopian sound and a much-valued sonic legacy. What helps Tovey's music stand out from the others was his use of nontraditional instruments. More so, it was the work and additions of John Fryer (producer), who is listed as adding extra fingers, ashtray, metal chair, and studio to *Fireside Favourites*. This, along with Tovey's use of similar instruments, including the electric shaver, allowed the album to sonically separate itself from releases within the genre in 1980, including Swell Map's *Jane from Occupied Europe* and Pylon's *Gyrate*.

The subject matter of 'noise' in electronic music production has been discussed previously with Attali's writings, and a more contemporary and social overview of noise in music is provided by Russo and Warner (1987–1988) in an article entitled 'Rough Music, Futurism and Postpunk Industrial Noise Bands.' They refer to the historical term and concept of 'rough music,' or 'charivari,' in that it was 'the name given in England for the practice of noisy, masked demonstrations which were usually held at the residence of some wrongdoer in the community...involving banging of saucepans, kettles, the rattling of bones and cleavers, hooting, blowing bull's horns' (Russo & Warner 1987–1988, 47–48).

Such events went on well into the nineteenth century, and much was born out of a sense of community shaming those who were wrong, and it in many ways formed a domestic hierarchy. Such a process was also popular in France, where it took positioning for mocking those who were in violation of community norms.

The area and study of noise, and its relationship to both social and community rituals, is very much in line (metaphorically) with Tovey's relationship and implementation of instruments that provide the same function; discourse and instability with the genre of music implied. Tovey's recorded output and his use of noise was a demonstration against the tempered scale, tonality, and Western music, of both signal and noise, and a misuse of technology.

*Fireside Favourites* is filled with electronic instruments that were available at the time. Tovey's route into electronic musicmaking was via tape machines and through non-instrument–based soundmaking, and his approaches to experimentation also mean that different forms of technology were Tovey's approaches to the physicality of music and his manipulation of its format, analog tape, that would be his first conditionings of technology, commenting:

> I had an old Grundig tape machine and I managed to discover a way of
> disconnecting the erase head from the playback head. I built a simple
> switch between the two, so I could decide whether or not the sounds
> already on the tape would be erased and I spent a while building up
> sound collages like that.[10]

Chris Watson similarly would go through the same experience, using the
tape machine as a conduit into other electronic devices. Again, Bowie, and
to a lesser yet no more important degree, William Burroughs, influences a
generation of musicmakers to experiment with the collage, be it auditory
or just with text alone.

Although Tovey had Daniel Millers Arp 2600 and Roland SH2, he
went alone without Miller on the recording of *Fireside Favourites*, a decision
that may have compromised the overall output and sound of the album, as
Tovey elaborates:

> I felt that I wanted to work on my own and in the end the end decision
> had mixed consequences. On one hand, nobody made decisions for
> me, so I was able to see through everything myself, which I think was
> important, but on the other hand, I was really very green when it came
> to how to go about recording in a studio. Blackwing was only an eight
> track in those days, but I still felt daunted by the equipment and looking
> back on it I did make a few mistakes that I wouldn't have made if I'd
> had someone knowledgeable to help me.[11]

The role of the producer is evident, or perhaps Tovey was aware that if
Miller was involved, in some way his stamp or signature sounds would be
compromised. Perhaps Tovey also underestimated what the studio would
provide during the compositional process. In *The Studio as a Compositional
Tool*, Eno was clever to notice that 'the recording studio allows you to
become a painter with sound, that's really what you do in a studio, you make
pictures with sound. Making records was quite a different way of compos-
ing from the techniques that we'd been used to in the past. This is different
from the old idea of presenting a record of a performance' (Eno 1990, 45).

Beyond *Fireside Favourites*, Tovey would become more interested
with acoustic instruments or the approximation of acoustic instruments
via digital synthesis as both *Under the Flag* (1982) and *Gag* (1984) would
employ. Eno perhaps sums up Tovey's approach and use of technology
in that 'the technologies we new use have tended to make creative jobs
do-able by many different people: new technologies have the tendency
to replace skills with judgement—it's not what you can do that counts,

but what you choose to do, and this invites everyone to start crossing boundaries' (Eno, 1996, 394).

## CONCLUSION

Two defining and more tactile elements (portability and the use of presets) allowed the user of the synthesizer to have more options for it to become a viable instrument of choice, and as Demers (2010) further explores, it began to change the production of electronic music, pointing out that:

> The year 1980 is a turning point for another reason. Although there are compelling reasons to respect the divides separating high-art from mass culture electronic music made earlier in the century, slippage between the two spheres began to accelerate after 1980. (Demers 2010, 9)

Tovey was in many ways caught within these crossroads, and his work was made and released during this change in the technological framework. As Demers points toward, it was also in lieu of changes in consumers' need (and want) to propel itself into the digital landscape of the 1980s.

Along with this, mass media outlets like television would go on to become dominant in the dissemination of electronic music, something on which Tovey just about missed the boat. A number of other factors are in play that can in many ways explain why today's music is not well; Mute Records (distributed via Rough Trade) was just starting out, with *Fireside Favourites* being only its third release. Lack of budgets and publicity meant that Mute was competing with major labels for space and content. Yet this cannot and must not alone explain why Tovey became a forgotten pioneer. It was the discursive nature of his music that meant he could only sustain a certain level of underground following, unlike acts like Depeche Mode, that would go on to conquer American audiences in the late 1980s. Furthermore, in writing this chapter, it was found that very little has been written about Tovey's work.

Ultimately, perhaps just being plain weird is not always a bad thing, as Fisher (2016) observes, in that 'modernist and experimental works often strike us as weird when we first encounter it. The sense of *wrongness* associated with the weird—the conviction that this does not *belong*—is often a sign that we are in the presence of the new' (Fisher 2016, 13).

## NOTES

1. See Cox and Warner (2005), 211.

2. See Cascone (2000), 13.

3. See Attali (1977), 51.

4. Ibid.; Cox and Warner (2005).

5. CD liner notes to Fad Gadget's *Fireside Favourites*, Mute Records, November 1980 (author copy).

6. Much of this process meant the dead could join others in heaven. See also https://www.pbs.org/mormons/faqs/ (accessed February 11, 2022).

7. See also Tovey, quoted in *Zigzag Magazine*, No 114, June 1981, http://www.bunnies.de/akiko/Music/interviews/fad2.html (accessed June 2, 2022).

8. See also Tovey, quoted in https://collapsingnewpeople.blogfree.net/?t=1837756 (Accessed May 6, 2022).

9. See Heidegger (1977), 22.

10. Tovey, interviewed in *Electronics and Music Maker*, April 1984. See also http://noyzelab.blogspot.com/2013/11/fad-gadget-e-interview-1984-dan.html (accessed June 20, 2022).

11. Ibid.

# III

## CROSSING THE MAINSTREAM

# 8

# THE HUMAN LEAGUE

## Electronically Yours

Technology and its effect on electronic music production has a duality and can be viewed as something that has had a liberating effect on electronic music production. However, this is also tainted with a pessimistic viewpoint, in its degrading of the music and/or musicianship of the player and the development of a mechanised and soul-less by-product. Goodwin (1992) points toward the production rather than the sound of what technology can facilitate, in that:

> There are clearly dangers in thinking about music as though it were a free-floating mystery, a social practice unconnected to actual conditions of production. As students of pop we need to know exactly how the means of musical production impact upon the sounds themselves. But in undertaking that task we have to recognize also that the definitions of music and musician can change. The new technologies of pop music have not created new music. But they have facilitated new possibilities. (Goodwin 1992, 97)

Production and process are deterministic matters, with one often facilitating the other. Into the 1980s, the advent of MIDI, although streamlining production and workflow, would further complicate the hierarchical division between making and producing, and this creation 'involves technological dexterity, but is not defined and determined by the technology as human beings are making deliberate choices about what sound right to them' (Longhurst 2007, 83).

Working-class identities feature within nearly all of the acts' documentation thus far, and such an influx of musicians crossing back to the 1960s with acts like the Beatles. Acts such as Cabaret Volatire are a far cry from the middle-class smugness from mid-1970s acts like Pink Floyd, and much of this identity is fueled by both antiestablishment attitudes and the invertable and inescapable extremes of poverty. George Orwell considered such conditions and their escapism with great attention in *The Road on Wigan Pier* (1937), and he saw that it 'involved is not merely the amelioration of working-class conditions, nor an avoidance of the more stupid forms of snobbery, but a complete abandonment of the upper-class and middle-class attitude of life' (Orwell, 1937, 161–62). Such manifestations continue today in musicmaking, although identity (through social commentary) has taken a back seat.

Whatever may constitute Englishness and Britishness was certainly bypassed by the Human League, an act that ignored the established ideals of popular identity and cultural expression to forge its own version of electrofuturism, steeped in a coldness that was (commercially) offputting for many. This chapter chronicles their background, influences, and use of technology, and it examines their seminal album, *Reproduction* (1979), which, after *Travelogue* (1980), would see the group change its lineup and direction toward a sound that would bring about a massive rise in popularity.

## INFLUENCES

James Joyce's modernist masterpiece, *Ulysses* (1922), ends with the line, 'Yes I said, Yes I will, Yes,' and in what at first may seem as just an abstract exposition, the sentence was full of foresight and the optimism of the modernist mindset. For many artists, Modernism (c. 1890s–c. 1950s) was a form of escapism through a changing world via the Industrial Revolution, war, and urbanisation. For Joyce and many other artists, the sense and needs of the individual were another key factor, in that this represented more interest than society as a whole. The more dominant strain of art movement that had come before it, Realism (c. 1840s–1880s), seemed now dated and obsolete. Here, everyday life was the subject matter, and with this realism, the sometimes dark and earthly pallets, which Realist painters used, confronted the ideas and ways of art's notion of beauty, the notions that every day and everything is beauty.

Modernism (music) came about via the reconsideration of the old forms of music and a move away from a more rugged tonality. Percussion was to now feature more heavily through this break from convention. Further to this, an emotional provocation was now at the core of this new musical movement, a movement that, like its counterpart in music, looks to express the mood of the modern age.

Botstein (2001) regards Modernism inherently progressive, in that:

Modernism, throughout the 20th century, retained its initial intellectual debt to Wagnerian ideas and conceits regarding the link between music and history. The art of music was perceived to need to anticipate and ultimately to reflect the logic of history. In Wagner's view, the imperative of art was a dynamic originality rooted in the past but transcending it. The history of music developed progressively through time, rendering initially novel and forward-looking styles dominant, only to witness that dominance undermined and superseded by the next wave of prescient change as history moved forwards. Success with the established audience of one's time was not a criterion of aesthetic merit or historical significance. (Botstein 2001, 2)

Composer Edgard Varèse (1883–1965) captured what Modernism brought about when he wrote: 'I dream of instruments obedient to my thought and which, with their contribution of a whole new world of unsuspected sounds, will lend themselves to the exigencies of my inner rhythm and the very newness of the mechanism of life is forcing our activities and our forms of human association to break with the traditions and methods of the past in the effort to adapt themselves to circumstances' (Varèse 1966, 11–19). The work of Varèse and the foundations of Modernism brought about an experimentalism in music that would go on to influence all and every form of music, including the underlying movinations of the Human League, which took elements from Modernism, mechanisation, and urbanisation as a starting point to create a truly unique and signature electronic sound.

Technological achievements in sound can be traced even further back as far as the World's Fair in Paris (1900), and the 'expositions encapsulated and celebrated the achievements of an industrialised modern society, inspiring artists, engineers, musicians, architects and many others' (Toop 2018, 20). During this period, film and the beginnings of avant garde music was taking shape as the Western world was steeped in its own progress, and as progress and modernism was closely tied to the development and popularisation of science fiction, Schmidt (2010) observed that it was 'born as a self-conscious literary genre somewhere in this time period, although it did not name itself until a few decades later' (Schmidt 2010, 26).

This exploration was also evident through sound, and if any one instrument would go on to define the 'sound' of science fiction, it was the Theremin. Leon Theremin, a Russian physicist and musician, invented the instrument, one that would break all connections to traditional instruments in that it truly represented the modernist world; it was at the cusp of radio broadcasting, and the idea that technological advancements were now accelerating at advanced paces. The fact that this instrument could be played without any physical contact was also something truly revolutionary. With no keyboard or fretboard, the instrument is played via the manipulation of an electromagnetic field around two antennae, one controlling pitch and another controlling volume. Theremin accidentally stumbled upon its creation while inventing a device to measure the properties of gas, and through this process, he observed that it created a low frequency whose pitch could be controlled by the movements of his hands.

As a trained musician, Theremin could see the potential of such a process, although not everyone shared this view, as:

> Not only for the physical coordination it requires to synchronise the hand movements around the two antennae, but especially for the demands made on the performer's sense of pitch. The player must be able to remember precise positions in three-dimensional space, without reference to frets or a fingerboard. Moreover, small inadvertent motions of the right arm will cause the pitch to fluctuate noticeably. (Leydon 2004, 31)

After performing for Lenin in 1922, it would be his time spent in New York City that would prove most rewarding, yet not without its consequences, as after nearly a decade of both public presentation and performances with his collaborator, Clara Rockmore and a patent deal with RCA to mass produce the instrument. Theremin was abducted back to the Soviet Union in 1938, where he was, at first, imprisoned, then hired by the KGB to make tapping and listening devices. It was only toward the end of his life, in 1991 at the age of ninety-five, that he would return to the United States for a series of concerts with Rockmore, and at the cusp of the collapse of the Soviet Empire, he would go on to see the impact of his device.

What Theremin had created was truly revolutionary, as it suggested otherworldly ideals: contacting the dead, outer space, and other dimensions. Its sound was also a complete disruption to traditional norms, and it culturally became associated with the sounds of space in films like *The Day the Earth Stood Still* (1951) and *It Came from Outer Space* (1953). Ultimately, the instrument represented a tool that allowed electronic sound to become devoid of classification, pitch, and convention, if only until the advent of the synthesiser came about.

## BACKGROUND(S)

Science fiction would also play a more influential role in popular culture, be it in perhaps a more lowbrow form of entertainment, via the board game. During the 1970s, the board game company Milton Bradley (MB) would popularatize this mode of entertainment throughout the globe. Beginning in 1860, in Springfield, Massachusetts, the company had their first successful game with the Chequered Game of Life in 1861. A variation of Snakes and Ladders, this game had players move along a track from early to old age. The cognitive power of the board game cannot be underestimated; the naval warfare game Battleship was a complex strategy-building experience. Players were tasked with concealing and defending their fleet of ships against their opponents. As a form of entertainment, the very physicality of the board game would become the basis of computer game technology, which would go on to replace much of the market during the 1980s.

Science fiction would become a very important target area for board game manufacturers who were keen to monetize on this wave of the popularisation of science fiction, and one such game was Star Force: Alpha Centauri, developed by Simulations Publications (SCI) in 1974. Designed by Redmond S. Simonsen, the game was made up of a collection of star systems with earth acting as its centre. Within one of these star systems was 'The Human League,' a society that seeked out more independence from earth.

Sheffield County Council is largely responsible for bringing both Martin Ware and Ian Marsh together. Meat Whistle, a youth theatre and art workshop group set up by the council in 1974, was a breeding ground for Sheffield youth who did not quite fit in. Set up on Holly Street, the initial grant was only for a four-month run, but its organisers, Chris and Veronica Wilkinson, ended up running it for over four years. For all people concerned, it was a place to experiment, where bands were formed and disbanded overnight. A number of seminal events occurred during this period. For many in the group—in particular, Ware—hearing Kraftwerk (via Cabaret Voltaire's Kirk) was a turning point.

Similarly, Punk gave rise to a spirit of independence, and the city offered, as Ware recalls, observing:

> Well, the North in general is like that but Sheffield in particular is a city of unexpected juxtapositions. Because part of it is good, honest, working class, put a lot of effort into it and it will sound great, craftsmanship and on the other hand, at the time, a desire to escape from the mundan-

ity from unemployment and a lack of prospects. Of course it's changed
now and we've obviously done a lot of recontextualizing of it over the
years but looking back now that seems to be what was going on. But
that wasn't what was driving us at the time. You just do it at the time.
You don't theorise about it. You just do it. In the fullness of time you
can analyse why.[1]

A computer operator by day, Ware had an interest in electronics and
electronic devices, and the first incarnation of the Human League, with
Ian Marsh, was the Dead Daughters. A combination of tamla motown
and avant-garde electronic music, the group didn't achieve much in their
short life span. The next variation, the Future, formed in 1977 with Adi
Newton, who would go on to form Sheffield's Clock DVA, was far more
formative. Although they released no material and had no interest from
labels, they did record demos that would only see the light of day twenty-
five years later, when they were released as *The Golden Hour of the Future*
on Black Melody Records in 2002.

These recordings are an amazing auditory document of what the
Human League would eventually form into, but far more sinister and
darker, with tracks like, 'Looking for the Blackhair Girls,' sounding just
as menacing as Throbbing Gristle's 'Persuasion.' The sense of comradery
and mutual support in Sheffield during the period of 1977–1979 has been
previously documented in this book, in particular, that of Voltare's studio
Western Works, which also acted as a hub of communities, in that:

> Relationships are better described as ambivalent and variable; some-
> times competitive, antagonistic and elitist; other times cooperative,
> friendly, supportive, generous, and mobilised by collective identification.
> Resources and favours were exchanged and this was crucial to the flour-
> ishing of both the world as a whole and the artist within it. Artists cannot
> go it alone—music does not work like that—and they know it. Whatever
> their differences, other artists and bands are useful allies and their common
> interests and involvement in shared activities inevitably generates empathy
> and friendship between them. (Crossly 2015, 7)

During the period of 1977–1980, the record industry was at a crossroads as the traditional models of recording, producing, and distributing
records were breaking down, and more and more innovation was now
being segmented into the hands of the makers, which, in turn, led to
changes in market structures, as Ross (2005) observed:

> Changes in market concentration lead to diversity in musical form,
> which in turn leads to musical innovation; this musical innovation leads

to market competition, which results in further musical innovation as each record company attempts to find a new musical form to stimulate consumer demand; innovation slows down as record companies strive to gain the largest share of the market for the most popular new musical forms (secondary concentration) and finally, this market concentration starts the cycle over again. (Ross 2005, 478)

During 1977, a collection of demos that were shipped around labels in London and to their loss, no one was interested, and Newton left to form Clock DVA. To both Ware and Marsh, it was apparent they needed not only more accessible songs, but also a lead singer who had some kind of unique contribution. At first, a mutual friend, Glenn Gregory, was the choice, but he was unavailable at the time. Ware suggested Phil Oakley, who was also at Meat Whistle, who was known not for his musical abilities at the time, but for his eccentric dress style around the Sheffield social scene.

Oakley's stylistic approach would be key to the early success of the Human League, and Eno (1996) observed some interesting relationships between the values of appearance and individuality, in that:

> Pop has always involved a melange of at least the following: melodies, sounds, language, clothes, fashions, lifestyle, attitudes to age, authority, relationships, the body and sex, dancing, visual imagery and the reassessments of value in all these things. (Eno 1996, 393)

Oakley accepted, and in mid-1977, the Human League (version one) was born. The same demos were repackaged and sent around to labels, again with 'Being Boiled' featuring as a standout edition. Somewhere between Kraftwerk and Funkadelic, its slow, hammering electronic percussion creates a stark and dense sound world while Oakley presents an array of lyrical subjects. With the majors still hesitating, the demos found their home in Scotland's Fast Products.

Released in June 1978 (and rereleased in 1982), 'Being Boiled' was truly unique, and like many other singles released by artists documented in this book, it failed to chart. Its liner notes featured a computer printout of the following: 'The League would like to positively affect the future by close attention to the present, allying technology with humanity and humour. They have been described as "Later Twentieth Century Boys" and "Intelligent, Innovatory and Immodest".'[2]

The single would go on to influence countless others to form their own electronic music outfits. DJ John Peel invited the group to record a version that was broadcast on the BBC on August 16, 1978. It appeared again in 1980 on the EP *Holiday 80*, where it would go on to have more chart success, reaching fifty-six in 1980 and peaking at number six in 1982.[3] Reviews were somewhere in between not knowing how to define the act and perhaps the most amusing was John Lydon's short July 1978 *NME* review of the single, in which he referred to them as 'trendy hippies.'[4] Bowie was far more complementary, referring to the single as 'the future of music.'[5]

*The Dignity of Labour* EP (April 1979) would portray a band that seems to go back toward more abstract and experimental material. Loosely based on a story of *Vostok*, a Russian spacecraft, and its astronaut, Yuri Gagarin, the four tracks (mostly composed on the Roland System 100) seem to be a step away from what had come previously. In any case, major labels were now looking at the act in a different light, and in May 1979, the band signed to Branson's Virgin Records. In a bizarre turn of events, Virgin had wanted to act and become more traditional and more commercial as a result. This process ended up producing their first single for Virgin, 'I Don't Depend on You,' which, due to its complete turnaround in both sound and style, was released under the name 'The Men' in July 1979. Having failed to chart, Virgin could see that a mistake had been made, and they allowed the act to continue on their own path, and what followed in August 1979 was their first album, *Reproduction*, an album that although perhaps devoid of humanity, the atmosphere and arrangements are truly futuristic, even by today's standards.

## BLIND YOUTH: *REPRODUCTION* (1979)

A central pretext behind this book is technology's role in facilitating the acts' intentions and secondly, for it to disrupt or break away from the traditions of popular musicmaking. For the Human League, image and the activities centred around this were perhaps just as important as Oakley, in his androgynous presentation, further challenged associated traditions. Through this, Oakley managed to obscure both contemporary place and identity to create an alternative image of the nation's future. At the cusp of the 1980s, perhaps it was time to do such a thing, to distance itself from its own past, as Rose (2011) suggests:

> The term 'national identity', as scrutinised by recent literary theory, has undergone a strange and uneven division of roles. Identity—as a psychic phenomenon in its coercive, self-contradictory ambivalent contours, or more simply identity gone mad—has taken off to the

post-colonial; while "national"—as in the cultivation of virtue and character—has tended to remain at home. So Englishness, while subject to
historical and political critique, has escaped psychic exposure. Or to put
it another way, in discussion of Englishness, relatively little has been said
about the potential insanity of moral life. (Rose 2011, 76)

To understand and detail what 'Englishness' connotates goes beyond the
aims of this book. However, the inception of the Human League represents a fascinating, if not psychoanalytical look into both the subjective
and individual sense of identity through musicmaking, one that would
become more evident throughout the 1980s.

This identity, aided by the associated technology (synthesizers) used by
the Human League, made a statement within sociocultural contexts, and as
Jones (1992) suggests, the sonic characteristics of popular music have been
informed by the processes and technologies of audio recording, in that:

> It is the technology of popular music production, specifically the
> technology of sound recording, that organises our experience of
> popular music. Popular music is, at every critical juncture of its history,
> determined by the technology musicians use to realise their ideas.
> (Jones 1992, 1)

The making of *Reproduction* was produced almost entirely by synthetic
means; hence, this is why it is a truly unique document of both composition,
arrangement, and performance. This process draws on a number of points
worth noting; the system in which it was recorded gives the record a
particular sound, and in the case of *Reproduction,* it was recorded in the band's
'workshop' or rehearsal space. The album was not recorded in a high-end,
technically complex environment, like a professional studio, and secondly,
the lack of live or acoustically recorded instruments (apart from Oakley's
vocals) extends both the sound and aesthetics of the album.

The album was coproduced by the English engineer Colin Thurston,
who had previously worked on 'I Don't Depend on You' and was perhaps
not keen to repeat the experience. His experience of working with Tony
Visconti on Bowie's *Heroes* (1977) and Iggy Pop's *Passengers* (1977) and his
relationship through producing Wire's second album, *Real Life* (1978), and
Virgin Records, brought him closer to the band. It's worth noting the role
of the producer here, often ignored as a core element of any production, as
Frith & Straw (2001) observed, commenting:

> I still think that record producers achieve a miracle every time they
> capture the spirit of a song or an idea; when they make it 'work' for

the rest of us who listen to the record; and that they will eventually be recognised as having been more important that many of the artists who received all the attention at the time. (Frith & Straw 2001, 119)

*Reproduction* has several distinct factors: Its rhythmic organisation, flatness (dynamics), and lack of silence and breaks makes it a very forward motion and continuous journey. The album opens with 'Almost Mediaeval,' and it begins with what sounds like a melodic motif of court music from that period, a pulsing krautrock beat, generated by the Roland System 100. Its tight, punchy, aggressive, and formal pop structure fools the listener into thinking that this is perhaps the trajectory for the entire album. It's certainly a take on the production techniques developed by Kraftwerk in Kling Klang Studios in Dusseldorf in the mid-1970s, but with a more distressed and dystopian slant, and its brutal and pounding electronic minimalism is not far off the work on Miller's *Warm Leatherette* (1978).

Further to this, it's a statement on musical and technological approach; with no traditional instruments being used, it perhaps signalled a change to this listener in that music can still be made upbeat and engaging without them. 'Circus of Death,' which initially featured as the B side to the 'Being Boiled' single (June 1978). More interestingly, the single version contains a more striking opening, as Oakley announces, 'This is a song called "The Circus of Death". It tells the true story of a circus we met. The first two verses concern the actual arrival at Heathrow Airport of Commissioner Steve McGarrett. The third emotionally describes a map showing the range of the circus. The fourth and fifth were extracted from an article in *The Guardian* of March the 19th, 1962. The last is a shortwave radio message from the last man on Earth.'[6]

The album version provides a shorter interlude with a voice over from LWT (London Weekend Television) presenter Peter Lewis, and it transitions into sound collage of recordings from recordings and announcements from Heathrow Airport. Lyrically, it presents a science fiction scenario in which the human race is poisoned by a drug called 'Dominion.' Unfortunately, the story is a surrealist tale that seems to end before it has begun. At only three minutes and fifty-five seconds, it seems unfinished, and again, musically, it's dark and morbid. The electronic percussion beats heavily, and the synthesizers dance around this with motifs of, as the title suggested, fairground tunes, although a macabre Human League interpretation of such. For Oakley, it was as much about being serious, but also playing on these ideals as this NME interview from March 1979 suggests, in that 'we're into cheap culture but not in a cheap sense. We respect our audience. We have to. If people come back a second time maybe they'll begin to understand that there is humour involved in what we do. But possibly at the moment we're not very good at putting it across. People think we're trying to be enigmatic. But we're not.'[7]

In the same interview, Ware gives some insight into, in particular, how the live rendering of works of *Reproduction*, considered now liberating synthesizers were to use, in that:

> Musicians do hate us. People want to surround playing musical instruments with a certain amount of mystique. All this 'we are better that you', there's no chance of us getting bogged down in technology and technique. We play our musical instruments because it's so easy. More people ought to do it. People should go out and buy their own synthesisers and create their own music.[8]

'The Path of Least Resistance' follows and again is minimalist, utilising a monotonous electronic percussion such a song would not feel out of place on the soundtrack for Stanley Kubrick's *A Clockwork Orange*. Lyrically, Oakley considers a mindless, controlled life, a life of ignorance and indifference:

So sad, the early grave,
When all the fun's for free,
Start digging the early grave.

Its apathy toward the listener is almost suffocating, in that what you have in this life is an early grave and its heavyhanded approach could fall apart at any moment, yet this is saved, musically, by its production, which much of Depeche Mode's *Speak and Spell* (1981) references.

'Blind Youth' is perhaps the track most resembling the established sound of another. Devo's album *Q: Are we not Men? A: We are Devo* (1978) sonically shares a number similarities, in particular in the electronic bass and percussion. The proceeding doom and gloom is replaced here now with the album's most upbeat number with Oakley singing: 'High rise living ain't so bad.' Oakley sounds more confident here, as his vocal range extends upward in pitch as compared to the more monotonous delivery thus received so far, and although it's tongue and cheek, it is perhaps the most coherent track on the album. So far the use of consistent electronic rhythmic patterns gives *Reproduction* a sense of immediacy and the consequence of this is a part of why the album is successful. As it breaks apart the mundane relations of daily life, we become aware of how both routine and time are inherently interlinked, and as Frith (1998) observes:

The individual and the social, the mind and the body, change and stillness and the same, the already past and the still to come, desire and fulfilment. Music is in this respect like sex and rhythm, is crutial to this—rhythm not as releasing physical urges but as expanding the time in which we can, asit were, live in the presence tense. (Frith 1998, 157)

Similarly, the rhythmic structure of 'Blind Youth' negotiates our experience of time and links us to aspects of both social and personal memory, and as Cohen (1997) considered this, as 'spatial-dynamics,' in that 'music fills and structures space within us and around us, inside and outside. Hence, much like our concepts of place, music can appear to envelop us, but it can also appear to express our innermost feelings/beings' (Cohen 1997, 286).

'The Word Before the Last' is one of the early pieces of the band that existed previously under the title of 'Again the Eye Again,' recorded as part of a BBC session recorded for John Peel in August 1978. We return to a slower pace of life, and it is a song that includes excerpts from television during the intro: 'You will notice that very appropriately I'm left-handed' and more fittingly, at the outro with: 'and described Mrs Thatcher's first three months in power as disastrous.'[9] Lyrically, it focuses on an existentialism that Oakley delivers, abstractly, singing:

The eternal moment laid bare,
No time to heal,
Continual pain, continual pain, continual pain, continual pain.

Surrounding these lyrics are synthesised melodies that are cold and distant, especially the electronic bass that stabs the air between the rhythmic elements. Monophonic instruments populate the album, and that is perhaps why the listener is left with such a black-and-white listening space, a space that draws on the power of minimalism.

'Empire State Human,' the album's single, released in October 1979 (and subsequently rereleased in June 1980), begins with an air of optimism, and after a proto-techno introduction, It's at full-tilt eight seconds in, and this sense of immediacy is one of the album's strengths; even though the lyrical and content are dark, the upbeat nature of the musical material (mostly) allows for a contrasting soundscape to appear dark yet light, and vice versa. Musically, it's perhaps the most simplistic presentation on the album as an electronic bass arpeggiation drives it forward, while a chime-like lead synthesiser line runs behind Oakley's vocals. Lyrically, Oakley considers how tallness (physically) leads to a sense of power and/or domination. This is presented through chant and repetition, as Oakley uses both 'Tall' and 'Wall' for musical punctuation. 'Empire State Human' did have commercial potential, yet it failed to chart on release, and as Ware explains, it was perhaps just a matter of the world being not quite ready, in that:

> I think everything we did at the time sounded alien and we wanted that, but we believed in our own ability to make that work and we liked it. We were encouraged by the record company and although it was still within our parameters, we honestly thought we had made a hit. So we basically wrote a nursery rhyme and made it quite fantastic in the literal sense of the word and Phil, to his eternal credit, came up with the words that were absolutely brilliant. The backing track is just great, but it was the classic right song at the wrong time.[10]

'Morale/You've Lost That Loving Feeling' is a song of two worlds. 'Morale' starts with a beautiful synthesiser-arpeggiated melody and sounds very much like the tones found on Japan's *Tin Drum* (1981). This is generated via Ware's newly purchased Roland Jupiter 4, and its sparse production leaves ample room for Oakley's vocals, which largely pertain to regret:

I don't forget,
The light growing weak now,
Experience is useless.

It is hard to pinpoint the content or subject matter of the song, and perhaps this was Oakley's attempt to abstract the listener away from it, and it is the only track on the album where he purposefully interjects rising dynamics (volume) and feelings into the vocals. However, at approximately two minutes, fifty-six seconds, ominous tones begin to appear accompanied with electronic metallic tonalities, and from this, an electronic bass line appears, followed by Oakley presenting us with a very famous opening line: 'You never close your eyes anymore when I kiss your lips.' In comparison of what has come previously on *Reproduction*, the inclusion of the cover version of the Righteous Brothers' 'You've Lost That Loving Feeling' (1965), is a truly baffling addition. Written in 1964 by Spector/Mann/Weil, Phil Spector's 'wall of sound' production is epic, as it is awash with reverb, giving it its angelic and ethereal sound. Not the case here, and in fact, the direct opposite as the non-use of reverb in this version makes it a very cold and lonely place. If the Righteous Brothers version is a rupture of emotions, the Human League's version is more reflective of a cold winter's morning.

Oakley's vocal presentation is deadpan, and it's the album's first duet, with Ware adding harmonies. One cannot help feeling like being in a karaoke bar while listening to it, and its daring arrangement makes it feels like it stands in isolation from the rest of the album, and perhaps the inclusion of this cover is a statement on the technology versus humanity ideal; a provocation and exploration of the mechanism of modern reproduction, one that is devoid of feeling and emotion.

'Austerity/Girl One (Melody)' again is a track that has two trajectories, a medley if you will. Firstly, it's upbeat and driving and has the same sense of immediacy as 'Empire State Human' in that it's mechanical and functional. The narrative of the lyrics have a duality as they deal with austerity and 'girl one.' The elders (or the austerity) cannot seem to get a grasp of youths and/or youth culture, and the daughter 'girl one' seems so very distant from their way of life. Again, the minimalist nature of the music or its backdrop allows Oakley to take centre stage, singing:

The father thinks in sadness,
On why his daughters went away,
On youth and other madness.

It's a tale of attempting to do your best, yet failing, and it's a story that perhaps many parents can relate to, losing touch with a child who is transitioning into adulthood.

'Zero as a Limit' ends the album with a dark and marching beat opening; the track takes quite some time to get up and running, almost two minutes, and is the most Kraftwerk-inspired track on the album, as it also uses a gradual increase in tempo, similar to 'Ohm Sweet Ohm' from their 1975 album, *Radioactivity*, although there, the Human League increases the tempo into an upward chaotic climax that Oakley has trouble, at times, keeping up with. Ware explains the concept behind the piece, commenting:

> 'Zero As A Limit' was always the track we finished our live shows with; we had this idea of doing a track that accelerated towards the end and that was the climax of our show. The contrast between the edginess and the live feel with the glacial emptiness is missing because the mixing and mastery didn't accommodate it. So the way we conceptualised it in the sequence, it felt a bit like a damp squib on the record.[11]

*Reproduction* captures the Human League, musically, between two worlds: both experimental and on the cusp of commercialism, and critically, the resultant outcome was largely misunderstood, as *Sound Magazine* of August

1978, where Chris Westwood contributes an uninspired analysis, in that: 'Simply, The Human League have adopted the synthetic/mechanistic disco stance and beaten Kraftwerk at their own game.'[12]

Andy Gill's review in *NME* in October 1979 was far more enlightening and considered not only the musical contents, but what Oakley was achieving, commenting:

> A lot of the blame for this lamentable state of affairs has to rest on the vocalist Philip Oakey's shoulders. As the possessor of a natural singing voice, he has the ability to give their material some emotional sting, to lend a sharp cutting edge of uncertainty to the ponderous inevitability of the music. But instead of feeling the songs, he runs through them: there's no projection in his singing, just enucleation. He remains restrained, impersonal, distanced from the subject-matter, unwilling to break the rules the way Sinatra, Crosby, Dylan, Buckley, Lydon, Presley, Waytt and a whole host of others did, and until he does, he won't come near recognising his full potential. The Human League story, so far, is one of missed chances combined with unclear thinking and lack of forethought. Rather than readdressing the balance, Reproduction only serves to throw their shortcomings into sharper focus.[13]

Although the album does have its faults, this would seem to be an overestimation of what the next album *Travelogue* (1980) would entail, an album that would be both Marsh and Ware's last before the Human League became household names. *Reproduction* remains a fascinating glimpse in a band pioneering their sound with technology and propelling synthesiser music into the next decade and is perhaps the all-encompassing dystopian sound of Britain at the cusp of the 1980s.


## TECHNOLOGY

Cultural theorist and critic Raymond Williams suggests that technology can and does affect the development of societal conditions and that changes in technology causes social changes, in that:

> The basic assumption of technological determinism is that new technology—a printing press or a communications satellite—'emerges' from technical study to experiment. It then changes the society of the sector in which it has 'emerged'. 'We' adapt to it because it is the new modern way. (Williams 1985, 129)

During the late 1970s, popular music making was adapting to the inclusion of electronic devices in musicmaking. However, minus technology, popular music presents us with the familiar, but it must also present us with something that will attract our attention, and this allows for its commercialism to appear. A distinctive character, front man, act or sound, will ultimately make it stand out from the crowd.

Popular music has traits that allows it to become easily consumable; limited vocabulary and well-defined musical parameters (verse, chorus, verus), and concealed inside of this is the power and potential of style and its marketability. As we have seen, the acts documented in this book were, in many ways, enslaved to technology, as it was a large component as to how the sound was produced and executed, and for many this alignment 'blurred the distinction between live and recorded sound, between musicians and engineers, between composition and performance, between the natural and unnatural noise' (Frith and Horne 1987, 174). The machines and technology they used not only changed the sound of popular music during 1977–1980, and the new classifications of electronic music production generated during this period can be broadly defined as follows:

1. Structure: use of repetition and minimalism
2. Timbre: little acoustic elements
3. Rhythm: electronically generated
4. Ensemble: traditional roles neglected

The Human League, which produced Britain's first album recorded entirely by electronic means, relied most notably, for the production of *Reproduction*, on the sound of the Roland System 100. Produced from 1975 to 1979, this semimodular monophonic synthesizer features on nearly all the songs. It consists of five modules: the Synthesizer 101, Expander 102, Mixer 103, Sequencer 104, and Monitor Speakers 109.

Mostly, the machine was used for drums and percussion sequencing via the 104 module. Ware comments on its use and the reasoning why they did not employ drum machines on the album, such as the Roland CR78 Compurhythm, which was available from 1978 onward. He comments:

> I was never really interested in that because we knew the uniqueness of the hardware sequencers that were attached to the System 100. We could drive everything off the CV/Gate and the timing was super perfect, we could have whatever sound we wanted on the end of those triggers. So it was more interesting to design your own sounds from

scratch rather than use a drum machine. My attitude changed about that when the Linn Drum came out in 1981.[14]

Further to this, Oakley expands on the use of the System 100 and further clarifies the manual use of the machine as the main percussion device, in that:

> This is what Ian Craig-Marsh used to use for our drums on the first two albums. He used to have it addressing the filter for both bass drum and snare sounds, and adjusting the timing with the second row of knobs coming out of channel B and going into the CV to clock. And that was how we did our drums—by ear. Ian had to have an amazingly fine touch just to get the intervals right.[15]

The Korg 700 was also another key synthesizer used on *Reproduction*, primarily on bass and lead lines. Due to its affordability, it was one of the first synthesizers purchased by Ware. Produced in 1974, it was a monophonic synthesizer that contained two voltage-controller oscillators and can be heard on tracks like 'Blind Youth' and 'Almost Mediaeval.' More so, it was the sound of 'Being Boiled,' and it was this machine that made the bass so distinctive on the single. Other instruments like the Roland Jupiter 4 featured on the album, but it was both the System 100 and Korg 700 that provided a truly unique timbre and sound world.

If we consider the milestones made by *Reproduction*, in the studio, this is where their contributions can truly be felt, technologically. Specifically, this is the space that inhabits where the synthesizer musician becomes the engineer, as they have the power and ability to shape and equalise their instruments before they reach a recording device.

In the production of *Reproduction*, Ware, Wright, Oakley, and Marsh distorted the roles of producer and engineer, as they, within their roles, as programmers and/or performer-programmers, fully illustrated that this new way of working, electronically, proved that both the technical and the aesthetic can work in harmony. Ultimately, the recording and production of *Reproduction* was a clear illustration of the democratisation of technology that allowed the Human League to create unique forms of expression, musical creativity, and sound experimentation, unheard of in Britain until that time.

## CONCLUSION

The popularisation of British popular music throughout the 1970s was aided and expanded by the mainstream media. *Top of the Pops*, which ran from 1964 to 2006, was a conduit for the expression of national identity through sound. In this, the acts that appeared, who were beamed into the home of millions of Britons per week, helped form identity and character for musical acts who were navigating through massive social, economic, and political upheaval. For acts pushing musical boundaries, the Old Grey Whistle Test on BBC2 would provide a much more significant platform on how its musical character was changing, particularly throughout the years of 1977–1980, as it focused on albums rather than the singles and chart areas that *Top of the Pops* broadly covered.

Bob Harris, its presenter from 1972 onward, would go on to leave in 1978 due to his distancing and dislike from the 'new guard,' which included Roxy Music and the New York Dolls. Reynolds (2005) observes 'as a distinct pop and cultural epoch, 1978–1982 rivals those fabled years between 1963 and 1967 commonly known as the "sixties"' (2005, XIV). Much of this musical discourse was exported to the world stage, in particular to the United States as Morra (2014) observed that 'the international reception and reputation of British popular music has enabled an overtly nationalisatic celebration of that culture and the national identity it assumedly articulates' (Morra 2014, 11).

The Human League, a small collective of musicians/programmers, disconnected themselves from past musical pathways, broke through and represented a significant shift in British music production. The sense of possibility delivered via the release of *Reproduction* in 1979 became the score of the possible futures for other acts to follow, something that very much distanced itself from the dominance of the traditional guitar, drums and bass format or what *NME* journalist Stuart Macoine observed as 'every generation throws four or five skinny young men, learning on a wall in a back alley, all cheekbones and self-possession and desperate glamour' (Macoine 2004, 243–44).

Cultural transitions came exponentially with the Punk movement, allowing for a reexamination of musical heritage. In the 1970s, others, like the Rolling Stones, would go on to use images and iconography from aristocracy, and John Lydon was quick to point out their distortions of both hierarchy and reality, observing:

> Music became as remote from the general public as you could possibly get. They became like little royal families unto themselves. They carted themselves around the country, waving to us occasionally. They bought immense houses, joined the stockbrokers' belt and sent their kids to public school. See? The system! They became it![16]

Oakley sang phrases on *Reproduction*, which sums up the unlimited possibilities of what the sound of the Human League represented and rather than an antiestablishment ethos, the Human League embraced progress, one that harnessed the nation's growing obsession with wealth, and as they moved toward a more technological-reliant 1980s, there was no more time for nostalgia or a harping back to the past.

In Sheffield in 1979, to the Human League, the past was dead and gone, and the future came from an intellectualist and individualist spirit of possibilities, free of traditions and imposed restraints. This approach, adopted by many electronic musicals discussed in this book, was partly due to the school systems failing to embrace and nurture the individual. Ultimately, the Human League produced a musicality that was facilitated through technological change, mediated by the use of the synthesiser and their music represented, as Morra (2014) eloquently argues a music represents 'the continuation of a tradition that enshrines the performance or pretence of rebellion within a proud heritage of contemporary national expression' (Ibid., 89).

## NOTES

1. See also https://thequietus.com/articles/04817-heaven-17-interview-penthouse-and-pavement (accessed August 3, 2022).

2. Liner notes to 'Being Boiled' single, Fast Products (1978), author copy.

3. See also https://www.officialcharts.com/search/singles/being%20boiled/ (accessed August 3, 2022).

4. See also https://www.fodderstompf.com/ARCHIVES/INTERVIEWS nmesingles78.html (accessed August 3, 2022).

5. See also https://www.heraldscotland.com/life_style/arts_ents/13124152. not-fade-away-1978-boiled-human-league/ (accessed August 3, 2022).

6. Author's audio transcription from 'Being Boiled' single, Fast Products (1978).

7. See also https://www.the-black-hit-of-space.dk/articles_1979_nme.htm (accessed August 5, 2022).

8. Ibid.

9. Transcribed by the author from the recording of 'The Word Before the Last,' *Reproduction* (1978) Virgin Records.

10. See also https://www.electricityclub.co.uk/martyn-ware-the-reproduction-travelogue-interview/ (accessed March 8, 2022).

11. Ibid.

12. See also https://www.the-black-hit-of-space.dk/articles_1978_zig_zag.htm (accessed August 25, 2022).

13. See also https://www.the-black-hit-of-space.dk/reproduction_review.htm (accessed August 25, 2022).

14. See also https://www.electricityclub.co.uk/martyn-ware-the-reproduction-travelogue-interview/ (accessed September 26, 2022).

15. See also https://www.soundonsound.com/people/phil-oakey-human-league (accessed September 26, 2022).

16. John Lydon, quoted in *Heavy Metal Britannia*, BBC, broadcast March 2010

# 9

## GARY NUMAN

## Subhuman in Suburbia

The equipment used in electronic musicmaking has become more readily available, and it is impossible to separate this progress from the people behind the machines, and as Brend (2012) observed that 'within this apparatus; there is a symbiotic relationship' (2012, X). Within the weight of the significance of the machines that facilitated this, we must always consider the humans behind them.

The work of the acts documented in this book are core to today's global electronic music landscape, and the current proliferation of these acts is largely due to the internet. Listeners, in an instant, are able to access early demos, thus being able to hear the incarnations of a band being created, piece by piece. In this, we can also hear the technologies of the past, and as Stubbs (2018) highlights, to what he refers to today as 'analogue vogue,' the means of production, in that:

> The tendency towards analogue and vintage electronics might feel like a passing fad, indulged by musicians and audiences of a certain age who would, if they could, opt out of the twenty-first century altogether. For them, these instruments represent more equitable, pre-neo liberal times, a period coasted, moreover in the grainy fuzz of nostalgic hankering for youth and a time when there was a future to gape in awe. (Stubbs 2018, 404)

The development and interest in our culture of 'analogue vogue' in modern-day electronic music production, points toward what Reynolds (2012) discusses as culture's addiction to things, in that:

> Is nostalgia stopping our culture's ability to surge forward, or are we nostalgic precisely because our culture has stopped moving forward and

so we inevitably look back to more momentous and dynamic times. (Reynolds 2012, 22)

Considering the past begs the question if we have now become 'culturally conditioned' in that, if through nostalgic approaches, synthesizers and electronics of the past become far superior to digital- or computer-based approaches. Reynolds continues:

> Not only has there never been a society so obsessed with the cultural artefacts of its immediate past, but there has never before been a society that is able to access the immediate past so easily and so copiously. (Ibid., 56)

Mark Fisher, along with Reynolds, refers to such processes as hauntology; a lost future that haunts society, a return to elements of the past, first introduced by French philosopher Jacques Derrida in his 1993 book, *Specters of Marx*.

Fisher, however, highlighted something core to the above discussion, and toward the era in which the larger discussion is taking place in this book, he observed that 'in the 1970s, certainly, culture was opened up to working-class inventiveness in a way that is now scarcely imaginable to us' (Fisher 2014, 26). With this in mind, this chapter examines the work of Gary Webb, as known as Gary Numan, his background and influences, and discusses *The Pleasure Principle* (1979), an album that crossed into mainstream and into the popular zeitgeist, a place where image becomes as much currency as musical progression.

## INFLUENCES

Defining the ideology and aesthetics of popular music is complex, and as its discourse is so varied, considering all its social and historical contributions, forming a singular definition is impossible. However Birrer (1985) attempted to do so with a summary of its main definitions, and it is documented as follows:

1. *Normative definitions*: Popular music is an inferior type.
2. *Negative definitions*: Popular music is music that is not something else (usually 'folk' or 'art' music).
3. *Sociological definitions*: Popular music is associated with (produced for or by) a particular social group.

4. *Tecnologico-economic definitions*: Popular music is disseminated by
   mass media and/or in a mass market (Birrer 1985, 104).

None of these definitions satisfactorily defines popular music, but they are at
least good conversation starting points. Take point four, *Tecnologico-economic
definitions*: This affects all forms of popular music and has been a commodity
from its very birth (c. 1798). However, what is important here are the institutional factors (record companies, TV and radio stations) that helped mould
early careers via the tecnologico-economic pathways, as without such, many
acts' beginnings would not have made such a successful impact. As the decade
of the 1970s ended, an array of genres was now at the forefront of popular
culture: disco, Punk, rock, and reggae. Many mainstream bands of the day,
including the Clash and the Police, cherry-picked musical elements from
each genre and blended them into a successful commodity. Again, Punk was
the channel that allowed for a new transition that came with the onset of a
new decade, when a number of subgenres were born, including new wave,
synth pop, and the new Romantic Movement.

Numan began his musical career with Tubeway Army (1977–1979)
and would go on to take a number of these genres as points of departure.
He used many forms, most notably alienation, as an aesthetic approach.
This was largely perpetrated via his cold presence onstage, a disconnect
from Numan himself. His work with the Tubeway Army would become
transitional, as it was 'hard rock with a futuristic sheen, rooted in the clean,
punchy riffs of glam' (Reynolds 2005, 323).

Yet, even from an early stage, he was branded as a Bowie ripoff, so
much so that Bowie's advertising for his 1980 album, *Scary Monsters*, came
with the tagline of 'often copied, never equaled.'[1] Bowie, suspicious of his
sudden rise to fame, weighed in on his opinion of Numan, as this *NME*
interview from 1980 suggests:

> Mac Kinnon: It's a rather sterile vision of a kleen-machine future
> again…
>   Bowie: But that's really so narrow. It's that false idea of hi-tech
> society and all that which doesn't exist. I don't think we're anywhere
> near that sort of society. It's an enormous myth that's been perpetuated
> unfortunately, I guess, by readings of what I've done in that rock area at
> least, and in the consumer area television has an awful lot to answer for
> with its fabrication of the computer-world myth.[2]

This sense of futurism for Numan was rooted in his interest in science fiction, with Phillip K. Dick being his greatest influence, as similar thematic

areas of relationship with postmodernism technology, alternate realities, and authoritarian states. Tubeway Army's debut, 'Listen to the Sirens,' references Dick's novel *Flow My Tears, the Policeman Said* (1974). While later Numan is referring to 'friends,' it's Dick's 'replica' or android from *Do Androids Dream of Electric Sheep?* (1968). The role of the replica (or replicant) is beautifully played out in Ripley Scott's *Blade Runner*. Produced by the Tyrell Corporation, these fictional, bioengineered replicants were genetically modified humans, although they are far superior as they have vast advantages over their human counterparts: speed and strength, to count a few.

The difference here is that in the novel, the androids are not so much not-human as they are inhuman, as 'the crucial difference is the ability to feel empathy' (Fitting 1987, 343), as Dick's novel points toward and this extract displays:

> He had wondered precisely why an android bounced helplessly about when confronted by an empathy-measuring test. Empathy, evidently, existed only within the human community, whereas intelligence to some degree could be found throughout every phylum and order including the arachnida. (Dick 3:27)

Some models of the replicants only had a four-year lifespan, and it was the job of the Blade Runner 'Deckard,' played by Harrison Ford, to hunt them down, as:

> Deckard is forced out of retirement to hunt and retire replicants against his will, while the androids themselves are nothing more than slaves; and Rachel is the product of a cynical psycho-technological experiment. Paradoxically, the film identifies and nourishes our fantasies of refusal and revolt against a system which uses and manipulates us, by allowing us to empathise for a time with the four androids and their desperate rebellion. But as they are retired one by one, the film forcibly reminds us of the futility of struggle. (Fitting, 348)

These dystopian ideals are born and conveyed within the songs, as the lives of these creatures within sprawling metropolises, and much of Numan's songs, often revolve around the following: isolation, disconnection, and paranoia.

Dick's influence on Numan is evident across a number of works. These aliens are categorised into a number of different forms: The 'friends' of 'Are Friends Electric' are cyborg buddies or sexpals; the 'Grey Men' perform the IQ tests that determine who is culled first; and the 'Crazies' are 'resistance guerilla hip to the machine's master-scheme' (Reynolds 2005, 324). Another elemental part of Numan's creation of his persona was that of the androgyny. This was by no means new, having already been tried and tested with great success by Marc Bolan and then Bowie.

Whereas the above used a more effeminate approach, Numan used disconnection and coldness as part of his visual language, which was further supported by his 'angular' use of the synthesizer. Numan was positioned at the forefront of this movement within popular music streams due to the commercial effect and appeal of his music. Yet, undoubtedly he was influenced by what had already come before, as Kraftwerk, the Human League, and Orchestral Manoeuvres in the Dark had already established themselves firmly. Numan was keen to use these machines to achieve an electronic sound that had a greater emotional involvement than the acts above. More so, it was through the very use of the instrument that Numan believed it would be possible to channel something more, commenting:

> By pressing one key you could unleash something you never heard before and then, by simply holding that key down, you could manipulate the sound and allow it to change. I became a firm believer in the idea that sometimes one note is not enough. Let that sound evolve–let that be the drama. (Numan 2020, 55)

Such statements validate the collective thinking and singular attitude adopted by the acts reviewed in the book, in that their music(s) was a rebellion of progressive rock of the 1970s, when the virtuoso approach was more dominant. The values and contributions of musical expression here become important, as any instrument can make a range of timbres and pitches, yet most are inherently limited. It takes the combination of both the composer and a mass of instruments (like a symphony orchestra) to extend the capabilities of musical sound. Composer György Ligeti achieved this in his piece *Atmosphères* (1961), where harmony, melody, and rhythm are disregarded in favour of what Ligeti terms as 'micropolyphonic'[84] processes. These mass textures become core to the piece itself, and ultimately the piece 'scarcely hints at forward movement. Rather the listener hears an all but motionless series of sound evolutions unfolding at various moments' (Woodstra, Brennan & Schrott, 746).

Perhaps unrelated, the piece highlights how the synthesizer is also capable of an enormous range of pitches, sounds unobtainable from any traditional instrument, and beyond the complexity and speed of human performance. The Moog synthesizer, or the miniMoog in particular, would become for Numan the vehicle for change and would help him reinvent himself.

Like Bowie, critics were quick to downplay, or strike off, Numan's ability to use both the visual and musical languages he was developing, as they were seen as a pastiche of what had come, or indeed, what was happening around him at the time, as this review of his album *Telekon* (1980) prescribes:

> All non-musical considerations temporarily to one side, I'd say that it was a woefully dull and monotonous album, pompous in the extreme and exceptionally limited in its range of tempi and tonalities (how a man who owns so many different synthesizers can be satisfied with so few noises is utterly inexplicable). His mannered whine drives me completely up the walls, and titles like 'I Dream of Wires' and 'Remember I Was Vapour' seem almost risible. Moreover, Numan's work seems almost entirely untainted by anything even faintly resembling wit or passion. (Murray 1980, 44)

While it is clear that Numan had a large collection of nonbelievers during this early period, his effect on the new metal scene of the mid-1990s, historically, is greatly acknowledged. Numan had actually announced his retirement after the release of *Telekon* in 1980, and then, bizarrely he 'rescinded on the decision, releasing a series of albums that saw him diversify his musical range but which were entirely eclipsed by the 1980s synth pop that actually came in his wake' (Stubbs 2018, 235). With all this in mind, Numan is key to the dystopian sound of Britain in the late 1970s, primarily in his use of science fiction as a route to mapping out the oncoming role of automation in industry during the next decade and indeed the reign of Thatcherism that would follow.


## BEGINNINGS


Gary Numan was thrust into popular music culture at the cusp of electronic music technology during the last year of the 1970s, and like many, the conditions and the limitations of traditional instruments (the guitar in particular) led Numan to the synthesizer. He essentially stumbled upon a Mini-Moog synthesizer while in a recording studio during the late 1970s, and he was captivated by its sonic expressiveness. Soon after, the machine helped him slip into the pop mainstream, and its sound led him to massive chart success in the UK with Tubeway Army's *Are Friends*

*Electric?* (1979) and Numan's *Cars* (1979) on Beggars Banquet Records. With this unprecedented success, Numan became the accidental synthesizer spokesman, recalling that:

> I went from having never seen a synthesizer before to becoming the number one expert on synthesizer in the UK. I had a number one electronic album and people were talking about me being an electronic expert and all that, and I'd only spent about eight hours with a synthesizer because I could not afford to buy one. (Numan, quoted in Collins et al. 2003, 92)

From an early stage, thematically, his lyrics involved the removal of the human through automation and robotics, and our overreliance on and love affair with the automobile. Although Numan's band did not fully become an electronic outfit, its sound went on to influence an array of new wave and synth pop bands, including Ultravox and Visage.

Numan's background is working class. He was born in Hammersmith and educated in the greater Surrey area. His passion for flying was induced by his father, who worked at Heathrow Airport, and during his teens, he enrolled with the Air Training Corps. However, it did not last, and a long array of menial and mundane day jobs followed.

Numan was gifted a guitar by his parents, and this rather revealing quote demonstrates that, from an early age, the search for new sounds always there, in that:

> If I'm honest, I was spending a lot of time not exactly playing it but plugging it into a variety of effects pedals and making noises. I was, even then, more interested in the sounds that instruments could make than I was learning scales and becoming proficient as a player. (Numan 2020, 15)

Numan began his musical career fronting the short-lived Mean Street, and shortly after, along with bass player Paul Gardiner, he formed the band the Lasers in late 1976. After shopping around demos and a rename to Tubeway Army, in early 1978, Beggars Banquet signed the group, and the single 'That's Too Bad' followed in February.

The song failed to chart, but it sold quite well considering its limited distribution. However, during this period, Numan questioned their adoption of Punk, where many bands had to navigate the grimy backroom pubs of London to make a name for themselves.

Such conditions came as part of the Punk movement, and the audience that came with it was confrontational and violent. For Numan, it was far too much to deal with, and at this stage, he decided the group would be far more suited as a studio-based project.

During July and August 1978, their debut album, *Tubeway Army*, was recorded at Spaceward Studios in Cambridge. It was during this period that Numan attempted to remove himself from both the Punk scene and indeed their sound. Numan suggested to Beggars that the band's name should be replaced with his new persona. They were not keen on the idea, however, and as such, it was rejected by the label. The single 'That's Too Bad,' released in February 1978, failed to chart and was not received well critically.

Although much of their sound was guitar-heavy, the MiniMoog synthesiser made its appearance on the single record. Much of Numan's early interaction with the synthesizer came from a similar aesthetic shared by other musicians discussed in the book, that of Punk approaches and aesthetics. Having no rules to play by, it was an open forum in which to explore the dynamics of sound, an open-ended platform in which experimentation played a major role, and much of the soundworlds created by both Numan, as he points out, came first by playing the MiniMoog. He comments:

> The room shook and you felt the sound as much as heard it. I had never experienced anything like it, and I was absolutely blown away. This was everything I'd been looking for. The sheer weight of the sound was shocking. It was like a huge bulldozer of noise, a vast wall of sound. It was a sonic assault on the ears. It felt unstoppable, immensely powerful and totally exhilarating. For me, everything changed in that one moment. (Ibid., 50)

Not everyone was fully convinced about this sudden change in musical direction, in particular his label, Beggars Banquet. This machine would largely dominate its followup, *Replicas* (1979); so, too, would Numan's interest in referencing science fiction, as lyrically, it's far more mature than *Tubeway Army* in that a lot of its content reflects his fascination at the time, including that of the man/machine principle. As the cover points toward, the androgynous look that Numan would adopt from this point onward.

Numan and his bandmates would be shocked, to say the least, with the success of the single 'Are Friends Electric?', released in May 1979. This would be their last recording under the name Tubeway Army. This was quickly followed by another single, 'Cars,' in September 1979, which went to number one in the UK and Canada. It was here that Numan crafted his sounds to make it his own. The following years would witness many changes, from flying a plane around the world and a number of subsequent albums that did not have the same approach or success as earlier releases. Numan's retirement from touring, the last of which saw three nights at London's Wembley Arena in April 1981, was perhaps ill-informed, as Numan was later reflective on the decision, contributing that:

> I really did believe that it was the root of all my problems, and I still believe that getting out was a wise decision. But what I should have done was just back away, given it some time, done some growing up, waiting to see how I felt in another year or two having not toured for a while. Making a big announcement like that I was going to retire was stupid and childish. But I was still so young, and the overwhelming effects of a rapid onslaught of a newfound fame were still raw and painful. (Ibid., 110)

Much of Numan's bad experiences from touring stemmed from the expensive tour rigs he employed during both *The Touring Principle* (1979) and *Teleklon* in his 1980 UK tours. The latter made use of radio-controlled robots, pyrotechnics, and a mass of articulated trucks to transport around. Moreso, Numan's leap into the spotlight simply put him in a position with which he was not entirely comfortable. This, coupled with his love for the studio and experimenting with sound, meant that touring became a chore for Numan. This would eventually lead to more expressive studio work appearing like the jazz and funk influenced *Dance* (1981) *I, Assassin* (1982) and *Warriors* (1983).

## REACTIONARY FUTURISM:
## *THE PLEASURE PRINCIPLE* (1979)

The work of the Belgian Surrealist artist René Magritte (1898–1967) took objects of the ordinary—such as hats, clouds, or apples—and turned them into the uncanny, placing them in the arena of the extraordinary. By 1926, Magritte began to reinvent himself as a figurative artist, and his most famous and instantly recognizable piece, *Man in a Bowler Hat* (1964), would become his most recognized. Although he had used the 'man in a hat' theme in other paintings, most notably, *The Son of Man*, from the same year, this piece is centred on the theme of obscurity, as the passing dove is 'snapped' and covers the man's face. This man, dressed in the uniform of suit and bowler hat, allowed Magritte to distort the everyday and dehumanise normality. Such a technique is used again in *The Pleasure Principle: The Portrait of Edward James* (1937).

James was one of the key patrons within the Surrealist Movement. Commissioned directly by him, the painting depicts an image of James, re-rendered by Magritte with the head missing, and in its place, a blinding white light. It captures the unconscious, although Magritte was weary of such interpretations, in that:

> The titles of pictures are not explanations and pictures are not illustrations of titles. The relationship between title and picture is poetic, that is, it only catches some of the object's characteristics of which we are usually unconscious, but which we sometimes intuit, when extraordinary events take place which logic has not yet managed to elucidate. (Levy 2016, 112)

Magritte's work is cinematic in nature, as objects and people often find themselves in scenarios that are mystical and thought-provoking. His work would prove for Numan to be a chance to explore, visually, the world of the solo artist. With this, he took *The Pleasure Principle: The Portrait of Edward James* (1937) as direction for the cover of 1979's *The Pleasure Principle*, an album that would now fully embrace synthetic sound worlds in which Numan attempted to present the future of pop as cold, dark, and oblivious to mainstream rock.

By July 1979, *Replicas* had made the number-one position on the UK charts, and Numan was in a very strong position career-wise after proving his worth to his record label, Beggars, both financially and commercially. Recorded at the now-defunct Marcus Music AB in London in mid-1979, *Replicas* saw Paul Gradiner (bass) and Cedric Sharply (drums) as now-permanent members. They would be core to the album's sound and key to understanding the album's aesthetics: Despite a focus on synthetic sounds, led by Numan, bass and drums are at the heart of this album, sound that Visage, the act reviewed in chapter 10, would follow on later that year. Perhaps it is this duality that made Numan as commercial as he would become, even though his lyrical disposition (isolation, paranoia, robots) was far from what would be primarily heard on the radio in Britain at the time.

The album opens with 'Airlane,' in what has been suggested as a nod toward Numan's flying career, as he had now obtained his flying licence. An instrumental at only three minutes, eighteen seconds, it introduces the listener to the album's sound world, with drums and bass playing a large, if not dominant role, setting the stage for this interplay between human and synthetic approaches. The lead synthesizer line, played now with the addition of a PolyMoog synthesiser, is to become the leading instrument on the album. Ethereal and part-symphonic, its proto-disco beat and bass ground the track as the synthesizers glide across them, and from here on in, the album's signature sounds is this created. 'Metal' defines this synthetic world in its opening melodic statement, and the sound of steel helps and aids toward the introduction of the other instruments. Soon the opinions of the android are apparent, as Numan sings: 'Plug me in and turn me on,' attempting to communicate the android's attempt to become human.

As referenced earlier in the chapter, much of this was borrowed from science fiction writing, in particular from Phillip K. Dick, and the sonic effects, like phase and flanging, are introduced here, giving the song an otherworldly feel. This helps create an almost ice-cold sensation, which allows Numan to communicate feelings of isolation and paranoia quite successfully. As a fan of Ultravox, Numan was no doubt influenced by their 1978 album, *Systems of Romance*, recorded with producer Conny Plank. Markedly different from Ultravox's earlier work, it brought synthesisers to the forefront of the group's sound. 'Metal' would have a new lease on life when in 2009, American industrial rock act Nine Inch Nails began to feature it in their live set, opening up Numan's music to a whole new (and much younger) audience.

From the very opening bars of 'Complex,' the sounds of Bowie's *Low* (1977) and *Heros* (1977) are evident, and the track would become the second single from the album, after the release of 'Cars' on August 21, to be released, on November 16, 1979. The piano and synthesizer duet open immediately, allowing the listener to understand that this is a more traditional approach to songwriting. Ultravox's Billy Currie adds violin and viola, and together with the reverberated and phased synthesizer, it paints a surreal and disconnected sound world, one slightly removed from both 'Airlane' and 'Metal.' Lyrically, it's a little confusing, as its subject matter can only be proposed, as Numan sings:

Please keep them away,
Don't let them touch me,
Please don't let them lie.

Such lyrical content could be directed toward anything or anybody: fans, the media, critics. Perhaps it is a more global statement on alienation, and to a lesser degree, states of paranoia, as Numan discusses, commenting:

> 'Metal' was about a machine created to be human-like but very aware that it wasn't. It was sad, frightened of the engineers who made it and confused by the fact that it cried without really understanding why. It

wanted to be human but knew it could never be and so could only look forward to a life of regret and disappointment. (Numan 2020, 76)

'Films' brings us back again to the dominant drum and bass format and is the most upbeat track to date. Again the PolyMoog synthesizer plays a central figure as lead instrument, and so, too, do the song's thematic elements, as Numan states: 'I don't like the film.' This idea of a 'film' could be taken quite literally; perhaps Numan himself is in the spotlight, as the line 'Turn off the lights' again perhaps points toward his view of stardom and fame. He continues with:

Now it's over,
but there's no-one left to see,
And there's no-one left to die,
There's only me.

'M.E.,' a track that has perhaps the most distinctive sound on the album, apart from, of course, 'Cars,' tells the story of the last machine left on earth. The machine has 'turned off' all the other humans, and he is the only one left standing. The dominant synthesizer lead line almost overwhelms the drums and bass, which almost seem to struggle at the 109 bpm. Ultravox's Billy Currie adds some violin to make this sound world seem a little more human, yet it fails, as the lyrical details, that of alienation and paranoia, seem to go directly against the opposing musical forces. Like much of Numan's work, the track would go on to have a new lease of life, when, in 2001, a sample of 'M.E.' was used by Basement Jaxx's in 'Where's Your Head At?' (2001).

In considering the cultural associations in which the synthesizer existed during this period, we see that Numan was using these machines to connect to another reality, and they were new and alien. As Rimbaud (2010) has suggested, synthesizers always expose the absence of the instruments they are supposed to imitate, in that:

Synthetic production presents cultural artifice, the sign, the map of recognition, as a substitution for the real, an alternative vernacular, 'as signs of the real for the real itself' as Baurdrillard argued. The erasure of historical reference points within this imagined synthetic universe has developed into simulacrum, which differentiates itself from representation in the sense that a simulacrum marks the absence, not the existence, of the objects it is supposed to signify. (Rimbaud, quoted in Demers 2008, 46)

This statement only makes sense when considered within a historical context, as 'some constructed electronic sounds are desirable because they are *approximations* imitations of acoustic instruments rather than faithful reproductions' (Ibid., 46).

Such contradictions appear on 'Tracks,' and its introduction, a blend of both acoustic and electronic instruments, is short-lived. What appears is another, almost floating and flying epic soundtrack. The combination of both electronic and traditional instruments here can appear now to some to be what you might call listening fatigue. Both 'Airlane' and 'Tracks' have many similarities; both use powerful percussion to drive the momentum forward. Numan's vocal presentation is somewhat muted, and the theme of 'Tracks' is hard to decipher as the lyrics seem to meander with a collection of unanswerable questions, as Numan sings:

Where are the tracks?
Where are the lines?
Where are the tracks, dear?
Where is the time?

'Observer' could be mistaken for 'Cars,' as it seems to be a melodic inversion of the letter's musical phrasing. A strong lead synthesizer takes the foreground, complemented by a phased and reverberated poly-moog. Here the protagonist is the observer, standing around watching, and perhaps it gives us a further indication of who is the voyeur, yet in such a short time for its theme to be established, vocals are only present from one minute, twenty seconds, to one minute, fifty seconds, and as per 'Tracks,' any subtext of an overarching message is hard to decipher.

'Conversion' has such a similarity in sound that it could perhaps be a reimagining of 'Observer.' Again, the theme of surveillance comes to the fore, as Numan presents: 'You're just the viewer, so cold and distant.' Structurally, it's more expensive than others, yet again it lacks the addition of a chorus, and this is perhaps what makes these songs so compelling; Numan is on the outside looking in, and as the album gets closer to completion, the songwriting quality reaches its peak, as 'Cars' no doubt demonstrates.

Released on August 21, 1979, the track would propel Numan into the limelight, including Numann's first US chart success. An ominous synthesizer intro leads us into what can only be described as a theme that is both memorable and recallable, which is provided by a PolyMoog with the bass line supported in unison by the Mini-Moog synthesizer. The machine/human duality is further supported with the addition of the live drums. Where most might have used a chorus after the first verse, Numan wastes no time in the delivery of its melodic content, and a two-bar phase is smartly inserted at an early stage. Mostly instrumental, the song ends in eloquent and blissed-out duelling synthesizer lines, washed in both reverb and phase effects. This is part of its commercial appeal, along with discussing a subject to which everyone can relate: the car. Whereas the Normal, as discussed in chapter 6, used the car as the subject of mechanophilia and death, Numan uses the car here as a place of sanctuary, a place of safety away from the prying eyes of the world, as the lyrics here confirm: 'Here in my car/I feel safest of all.' Numan also used the car to protect himself from society in general, along with a nod to Kraftwerk's 1977 homage to motoring, 'Autobahn,' a symbol of mobility and freedom. What separates Numan's and Kraftwerk's vision of the car is that the latter saw a fusion and idealism between nature and technology, but for Numan, the car was a place to protect oneself from society in general.

Like many other tracks on *The Pleasure Principle*, 'Cars' would have many new leases on life. It was used in commercial advertising works, including American Express and Carling Lager, but it would reach even further when Nine Inch Nails included it in their live set, introducing and exposing Numan to a whole new audience and level of appreciation.

The album ends with 'Engineers,' a strict marching-tempo song that counterbalances thematic elements while Numan contemplates, lyrically, a final dystopian message, singing: 'All that we know, is hate and machinery.' Thematically, it is an odd way to end an album of such contradictions, surrounded by the sounds of electrification and industrialization. *The Pleasure Principle* put Numan on the map, and the album helped alter the public's perception of the synthesizer, as even though there is an overreliance on the synthetic instruments used, the interplay with the human elements (drums and bass) really are also core features of the album.

Numan's thematic ideals of coldness, disconnection, and alienation centrally reflect the climate of late-1970s Britain, a time in which the separation of both public and state was cold, distant, and beyond reflection of reality. It is this iciness that proves to be the album's most successful trait, and it encapsulates the man-machine paranoia. With the lack of deviation (sonically), it's an album that has stood the test of time, even though Numan used the themes of Phillip K. Dick and other science-fiction writers to escape the mundane reality of a changing world. Ultimately, with *The Pleasure Principle*, Numan used electronic means in an attempt to make popular music more ambitious, more epic, and more reflective of a technological-driven world.

## TECHNOLOGY

Whereas other acts documented in this book exploited both homemade electronics and more affordable synthesiser brands (Roland, Korg), it is no understatement that the success of Numan's sound was derived primarily from the Moog synthesizer, and moreso, the MiniMoog Model D and the addition of the PolyMoog. Indeed, much of Numan's use of these machines was only facilitated by his request to the record label to have them initially rented during studio sessions, as they were horrifically expensive at the time. It would seem, as Brend (2012) suggests, resistance was still evident, in that:

> There was a lingering suspicion and sense of otherness surrounding the music. Critics continued to routinely air all the time-honoured worries about machines taking over, musicians being out of work, of music losing its soul. There was no eureka moment in between, just a speeding up of the advance of the art and the apparatus. (Brend 2012, 209)

RA Moog Co. began its life in 1954, when nineteen-year-old electronics enthusiast Bog Moog began selling Theremin kits. Composer Herb Deutsch asked Bob Moog to build something to create complex and experimental sounds, tones not easily created by other instruments or with studio trickery. The development of large-scale modular synthesizers saw them be used by sound research departments in US universities and by the few composers who could afford them, Wendy Carlos being one of them.

As discussed in chapter 3, the release of *Switched on Bach* (1968) would alter the public's perception of the synthesizer and throw it and an unsuspecting Wendy Carlos into the limelight. Even with this success, public perception was still at a low, in particular the musicians union in the United States, where 'the Moog synthesizer was for a time banned from use in commercial work. This restriction first surfaced in a contract negotiated between the American Federation of Musicians (AFM) and advertising agencies and producers in New York City in 1969. The union was worried that following on from Carlos's success, the synthesizer was going to replace musicians' (Pinch & Trocco 2002, 168).

Simple economics would keep much of both the musical community and electronics enthusiasts away from Moog. This was supplemented, in the United States initially, with the release of the ARP 2500 in 1970. Although still expensive, the 2600 model that came in 1971 provided a smaller, more mobile version of the 2600. However, even as Moog was busy developing the MiniMoog Model D, by the late 1960s, the company was losing money. Moog engineer Bill Hemsath developed a prototype, but with Moog being slow at first to see its potential, the company struggled to get the model off the ground and release it in 1970. Thirteen thousand Model Ds would be produced between 1970 and 1981 (Ibid., 215).

One of the original MiniMoog engineers, Jim Scott, reflected on its unique character, commenting:

> It was something like vacuum tubes, in that the circuitry would not suddenly go into clipping, it would distort gracefully.... Also, the circuitry was inherently wide band.... It passed frequencies far beyond the audio range.... And we're getting into guess work here, but the feeling is that there were things that happened up in the ultrasonic range that can cause inner modulation and distortions, [this] reflects back and can be heard in the audible range. (Scott, quoted in Pinch & Trocco 2002, 252)

Struggling to keep up with demand for the production of the MiniMoog, the company would be sold to a venture capitalist in 1971, and although they went on to make numerous models, including the PolyMoog (1975–1980), the MicroMoog (1975–1979), the MemoryMoog (1982–1985), the Prodigy (1979–1984), and the Rogue (1981), under financial difficulties, the copyright of their name brand would end up in the most unlikely place in the early 1980s: Caerphilly, Wales, under the ownership of Alex Winter, who would go on to produce the MiniMoog 204e[3] in 2003.

This machine would blueprint the sound of 1970s soul and funk music in the United States, through Stevie Wonder, Herbie Hancock, and Parliament. Even the great jazz astral traveller Sun Ra would go on to use it as an early test user of the machine. However, it would be its use in progressive rock, through Rick Wakeman of YES and Keith Emmerson of Emmerson, Lake and Palmer, and via Kraftwerk, Tangerine Dream, and Giorgio Moroder, that would allow Numan to first hear its signature sound. And it would indeed become a core part of his commercial sound, thus facilitating this crossover into the mainstream.

## CONCLUSION

Marxist theorist Guy Debord, who would go on to be instrumental in the formation of the Situationist International Movement, and who in turn provided great influence to Throbbing Gristle, coined the term 'psychogeography' in 1955. The area examines our psychological experience of the city, highlighting elements of a landscape, within a city, for example buildings of forgotten and discarded times.

London during the late 1970s was a tale of two cities, both Victorian and brutalist,[86] just at the onset of the 1980s, when it became transformed, architecturally, by both financial and technological change. Michael Bracewell's *Souvenir* (2021) eloquently paints a picture of London in the late 1970s and expresses how, here at the twilight of one era and the dawn of another, the city was transforming, transformed. The city had an aura, an atmosphere of change, in that:

> Oxford Street—the shabby end—the busy shops are ablaze with light: window displays, interiors and entrances, each asserting a world—all new and white, yet already worn-down thoroughfares, makeshift, scuffed and flimsy. Gloss-black mannequins, gunmetal cassette players, dancewear and album sleeves. Cosmetics and electronics, books and shoes; then the blank facade of a band and the dank yeasty smell of a pub.... And the steady crowds and the ceaseless shuddering lines of traffic: headlights and brake lights, the beginning of a fiune sleet blowing across the beam. (Bracewell 2021, 6)

This vivid portrayal of a city is a window into Numan's world, and it is brutalist in so many ways. With tracks like 'Cars' and others, he managed to hone into collective feelings of society's apparitions and fears—past, present, and future—all at the cusp of the oncoming digital capitalism that would wash over London in the early 1980s. Numan's creation of a 'reactionary futurism' in sound is, as Fisher (2013) points toward, 'long since ceased to refer to any future that we expect to be different' (Fisher 2013, 9). Even with this sense of foresight and with the themes he tackled, Numan was slated by the press as he pursued these ideas in later albums like *Dance* (1982) with Richard Williams of the *Times* of London describing it as 'irredeemable nonsense; not even funny anymore.'[4] Numan, however, did suffer from a very sudden swing into the highlight, and perhaps it was this immediacy of fame that made the reviewers take such a hardline, observing that:

> My rise was sudden, meteoric almost. I was totally unprepared for the reality of fame, and I had no experience of anything. I was young, naive and with a mental condition that, although I would never wish to change it, was crashing around in my head like a wounded elephant. I would not recommend that I made it to anyone, not that we ever really have a choice. (Numan 2020, 75)

His musical career throughout the remainder of the 1980s would be varied. He collaborated most notably with Bill Sharpe as 'Sharpe and Numan,' releasing the single 'Change Your Mind' in 1985. As the decade came to a close, the low-charting releases in the States with I.R.S. Records, *Metal Rhythm* (1988), and the Sharpe and Numan LP *Automatic* (1989) on Polydor Records, positioned Numan unfavourably career-wise. However, the next decade saw Numan finally gain more acknowledgement worldwide from endorsements from acts like Fear Factory, Nine Inch Nails, and the Nu-Metal movement.

In its exploration of what the future would bring, *Intruder* (2021) sees humanity now not as the domination and/or alien of the world, as per *Replicas* (1981), but as the destroyer and self-destructor. Nineteen albums into his career, Numan has contributed a wide body of work, more so than any other act reviewed in the book. Perhaps now part formulaic, what Numan delivers throughout his discography is this: a reliable and focused exploration of futurism and apocalyptic moods and atmospheres, be it a more controlled sense of paranoia, and perhaps what stands to Numan is his long-standing vision, even in times outside of the mainstream, and a sense of despair, to which he now, perhaps, is willing to surrender.

## NOTES

1. Advertisement. See also https://eil.com/shop/moreinfo.asp?catalogid=663174 (accessed July 11, 2022).

2. See also http://www.bowiegoldenyears.com/press/80-09-13-nme.html (accessed July 20, 2022).

3. For further information, see: https://www.soundonsound.com/reviews/moog-minimoog-204e (accessed May 15, 2022).

4. See Sutton (2016), 63.

# 10

# VISAGE

## The New Guard

Hebdige (1979), in *Subcultures: The Meaning of Style*, defined *culture* as an organic society in that:

Culture is a notoriously ambiguous concept as the above definition demonstrates. Refracted through centuries of usage, the word has acquired a number of quite different, often contradictory, meanings. Even as a scientific term, it refers both to a process (artificial development of microscopic organisms) and a product (organisms so produced). (Hebdige 1979, 5)

The formation of any subcultural movement is interdependent on many factors, and from traditional movements come new and alternative modes of expression. Hebdige (1979) pointed out what Punk brought about and explained how 'punks were not only directly *responding* to increasing joblessness.... They were dramatising what had come to be called "Britain's decline" and had "appropriated the rhetoric of crisis which filled the airwaves and editorials throughout the period and translate it into tangible (and visible) terms"' (Ibid., 87).

Punk dramatised many political and economic events throughout the 1970s, which was influenced by media induced 'moral panic' and political campaigns. All this further cemented Punk's being labelled a conflicted subcultural movement, and as Osgerby (2013) suggests, the media played on this and used Punk as a conduit to fan the flames, observing:

Rather than simply reacting to an existing condition of tension and anxiety, therefore, these responses can be seen as strategies that actively sought to bring about such a condition, deliberately heightening a sense of apprehension as a means of garnering attention and support. (Osgerby 2013, 202)

Visage would use fashion and changing societal and cultural ideals to form a sound that was a departure from the dystopian, using elements and notions of grandeur and escapism to create *Visage* (1980), an album that paved the way and produced a road map for the next generation of electronic musicmakers to follow.

## INFLUENCES

Figures and acts documented in this book have used major art movements (Surrealism, Dadaism) as points of influence for either aesthetics and/or performative approaches. For Visage's Steve Strange (1959–2015), it would be a mixture of fashion and futurism that would inform not only the music but more importantly, stylistic elements of what Visage's aesthetic would evolve into. As such, a number of influences are presented here for discussion and consideration.

Dandyism, or in some fields 'Eccentricity,' traces its roots back to the mid- to late 1880s, when certain men were known for a certain style of dress. To be 'dandy' was in many ways to be a person who placed significant importance on his appearance. Often of middle-class stature, a 'dandy' would often be seen attempting to appear as part of the aristocracy. Baudelaire (1970) observed this as:

> Dandyism appears above all in periods of transition, when democracy is not yet all powerful, and aristocracy is only just beginning to totter and fall. In the disorder of these times, certain men who are socially, politically and financially ill at ease, but are all rich in native energy, may conceive the idea of establishing a new kind of aristocracy, all the more difficult to shatter as it will be based on the most precious, the most enduring faculties, and on the divine gifts that work and money are unable to bestow. Dandyism is the last spark of heroism and decadence. (Baudelaire, quoted in Hauk 1997, 28)

The aesthetics of living, a romantic notion of life, one for which Lord Byron and Oscar Wilde would become most famous, would become popular within literary circles. More contemporary examples, as per George Walden's essay 'Who's a Dandy?' (2002), points toward both Andy Warhol and Quentin Crisp, while musically, Dandyism can be traced back to the roots of Glam rock (c. 1971–1975). As Glam Rock swept across Britain (c. 1971–1975), it represented a cross-segmentation of influences from popular culture: science fiction, 1950s rock and roll, and much more. It relied on fashion as its main conduit, with platform shoes, makeup, and questionable hairstyles all playing their part. Moreso, Glam Rock paved the way, perhaps for the first time in popular music culture, toward the look of androgyny, a more fluid and playful approach to gender roles, often played, quite convincingly, by heterosexual males. Much the same as Dandyness, Glam Rock celebrated the extravagant, the decadent, unlike the macho approach of 1960s rock, and within this, both Marc Bolan and David Bowie stand tall in the lineage of influence. Bowie, as Ziggy Stardust (1972–1973), as Bennett (2017) points out, stood out from the surrounding competitors, in that:

> The Ziggy image was undoubtedly deeply inspired by the visual indulgence of glam while also referencing Bowie's interest in science fiction themes, comic books and Kabuki theatre. While a more studied take on the glam image, and one that began a career-long obsession for Bowie in combining highbrow and lowbrow taste, Ziggy's image melded seamlessly with those of other glam artists of the day.[1]

Terrestrial television would again play a huge part in the distribution to the nation of Glam Rock's expedition of new styles and musical adventures. The fateful evening of July 6, 1972, would go down in popular music history, when Bowie performed 'Starman' on the BBC's Old Grey Whistle Test, a performance that would go on to inspire countless thousands to either change with current fashion, form a band, and/or completely change and alter its direction. *Guardian Magazine* features writer David Hepworth saw this moment as pivotal, in that:

> That was the moment Bowie went above ground and nationwide. The hype may have led us to expect something edgy and challenging. The record was as simple and hummable a radio hit as you could possibly desire. For the post-Beatles generation coming into their albums-buying majority, the record wasn't really the point. The point was the way he looked at them.[2]

Further to this, Bowie seemed to be intentionally, as Hepworth observed, pointing at the viewers, directly looking down into the camera and singing the lyrics: 'I had to phone someone, so I picked on you.'[3] As Marc Bolan was priming the nation with a string of hits in the charts during 1971 with 'Hot Love' and 'Get It On,' Bowie was exploring fashion sensibilities via

Fred Burrett, or Freddie Burretti as his persona called him. They ran into each other at the Sombrero, a gay club where Bowie would drink by influence and reference from Hollywood drag queens and fashion freaks and geeks.

Not only would Fred influence Bowie's style, but he became part of his temporary band, Arnold Corns Band, formed due to legal reasons. Burrett would remain at the side of Bowie from *Diamond Dogs* (1974) right through to his 'Plastic Soul' period (1974–1976).

Additionally, as discussed previously, another terrestrial television was evident as seminal in the influence and formation development of a more opulent and indulgent form of synthesiser music during the late 1970s. Roxy Music's appearance on the Old Grey Whistle Test in June 1972 (a month shy of Bowie's appearance), an art school sonic experiment, was beamed into millions of home, and as Phil Manzanera, guitarist for the band, fondly recalled: 'a lot of people say to me, the first time I saw you on Top of the Pops, I realised there's hope for a person like me, in Sheffield or Scunthorpe or wherever.'[4]

## BACKGROUND(S)

As the 1980s hit, the legacy and influence of acts discussed in the book was beginning to appear. All around the country, new acts, and in particular, new clubs began to act like cultural hotspots, where fashion and trends would be as quickly formed as they were denounced, as Steve Dagger (Spandau Ballet) fondly recalls:

> In early 1980, I heard there was another group in Birmingham: Duran Duran. As I perceived it, they had a disadvantage as they weren't in London. My whole thing was we had to be quick because there were starting to be a lot of others. There were similar sorts of clubs start- ing to be a lot others. There were similar sorts of clubs in every big city—you had Pips in Manchester, The Rum Runner in Birmingham, Maestro's in Glasgow, Valentino's in Edinburgh and there were various clubs in Sheffield. The idea of playing keyboard-orientated electronica came from those clubs. And so it was very quick. Some of those bands already existed—Depeche Mode. We [Spandau Ballet] had the first hit record, but we were followed very quickly by Duran Duran and also by Visage, Soft Cell, but I wasn't in the least surprised. (Dagger, quoted in Jones 2020, 140)

Strange, before his fame in Visage, started out promoting punk concerts in his hometown of Caerphilly, Wales, which eventually led to a key
position of cultural power: working for Malcom McClaren in London in
1977. His first act, the Moors Murderers, included an array of future stars,
including Chrissy Hynde, but it failed to make any real inroads musically, as a review by Andrew Gallix from *Sound Magazine* suggests: 'The
band played the Roxy on 13 January 1978, supporting Open Sore. Steve
Strange was on vocals (calling himself Steve Brady) and Hynde was on
guitar. Bob Kylie (Open Sore): They were terrible! Absolutely dreadful!
On 28 January 1978, Strange told Sounds that he had left the band.'[5] It
was Strange's interaction with Rusty Egan (then drummer with the Rich
Kids) that would become most influential, essentially kicking off the New
Romantic Movement from a basement bunker in London's Soho, where
the pair hosted a David Bowie night, aptly named 'A Club for Heroes.'
At Billy's, attendees were exposed to the mechanics of Kraftwerk, the cold
steel of the Human League, and the magic of Giorigio Morroder, and soon
Billy's became the epicentre for this new movement, as Gary Kemp from
Spandau Ballet recalls: 'The first time we went to Billy's, Steve Dagger said
we should go and get some synthesizers' (Kemp, quoted in Jones 2021,
140). Writer and academic Iain R.Webb recalls what Billy's provided and
represented for youth culture:

> The whole thing was about reinvention is very important, plus the fact
> that it all grew out of punk, which a lot of people don't think it did.
> You have to remember London was very grey at the time, grey and
> bland and conservative and locked down, and there weren't the outlets
> for people there are now. The New Romantic idea, with its flounces
> and the big bows and the crimped hair, was a reaction to our surround-
> ings as much as anything Self-expression through adversity. (Webb,
> quoted in Jones 2021, 200)

So much so was the importance of the movers and shakers of Billy's that
Bowie himself was an attendee, and on one occasion there, he picked
extras (including Strange) to feature in the music video for 'Ashes to
Ashes' (1980).

Between 1979 and 1980, Billy's moved to the Blitz Club, on Great
Queen Street, Covent Garden, London, and it would become a subcultural
magnet where both the sound and the style of the New Romantic Movement formed. In this new home, Strange, who manned the door, had a
strict entry policy, in that: 'I ran a very tight ship in terms of door policy. I
wanted creative-minded pioneers there who looked like a walking piece of

art, not some drunken, beery lads. The best move I made was turning Mick Jagger away at the door. He was wearing trainers' (Strange, quoted in Jones 2021, 197). More importantly, its core attendees, referred to as 'The Blitz Kids,' and who included Boy George, Midge Ure, and Barry Adamson, would have a monumental effect on the fashion of the New Romantic Movement. Here, fantasy, escapism, homemade costumes, makeup, and a highly androgynous style distinctly announced that Punk's more stringent uniform and look was now officially dead, and a article from the *Daily Mirror* featuring writer Christiana Appleyard announced that the Blitz Kids were 'the new wave that even made punk look normal.'[6] The period of the Blitz was also soundtracked, not only by Bowie and others, but by the group of which both Strange and Egan were a part. Visage and their breaking into the charts in 1980 can be viewed as a monumental shift as the role of the synthesizer changed, bringing about the sound of a more a more open-ended and optimistic future.

It was Ure and Egan who essentially began Visage as a studio project, as they were keen to play original music, with the intention of playing in clubs like the Blitz. Both were still part of the Rich Kids, formed by ex–Sex Pistols Glen Matlock in 1977, along with guitarist Steve New. Their debut album, *Ghosts of Princes in Towers* (1978), while well received, failed to gain any real momentum. The real breaking point came when a synthesizer, a Yamaha CS50, appeared within the band. Although both Ure and Egan were keen to incorporate it, Matlock and New were not as motivated. They preferred the power pop direction, as Ure elaborates, in that: 'Technology broke us up in the first place, when I bought a synthesiser, which Glen and Steve absolutely hated. Would I be going against everything I stood for back then?'[7] This eventually led to the band's breakup, and during this period, Ure and Egan had recorded demos, including 'The Dancer,' which featured on Visage's debut album. Egan suggested Steve Strange as frontman, as his flamboyant persona would certainly fit the role, and along with core members Billy Currie (Ultravox), John McGeoch (Magazine), Dave Formula, and additional musicians Chris Payne and Barry Adamson, the lineup fluctuated throughout the period of the group.

It would be producer Martin Rushent (1948–2011) who would be the first to both demo and finance their first recordings. Their first single, 'Tar,' released in November 1979 on Radar Records, was as much of a public service announcement as a traditional song, as lyrically it was about the dangers of smoking. The single did poorly on release, but in parallel, between late 1979 and 1980, at Genetic Studios, the band, now on Polydor Records, recorded their debut album, which included the single 'Fade to

Grey,' and when it was released on November 14, 1980, it shot them to success and fame, reaching the Top Ten in the UK and number-one positions in Germany and Switzerland.

Unfortunately, this fame was not built to last. Essentially a studio-based project, the recording of the second album, *The Anvil* (1982), would see many of the original members departed, as Ure had decided to spend more of his time developing Ultravox, of which he was now its front man and dealing with the fallout of their hit 'Vienna' (1980). Creative and personality differences between Strange and Egan also led to a split. Ure described this breakup as a combination of time and too many strong personalities, in that:

> The trouble with Visage was that there were too many chiefs, six characters all wanting an equal say without putting in an equal amount of work. I was doing most of the writing and producing, and we all knew Steve [Strange] was the frontman, but when it became successful, jealousy and the nasty side of the business crept in. That was never the way it was intended.[8]

Visage would continue to operate throughout the 1980s, but with Strange's battle with heroin addiction and failing chart success, the impetus and immediacy of the first album became hard to match. Like many acts discussed in the book, Visage would have a second life, and a whole new generation would appreciate their sound in the 2000s when they reformed and toured, albeit with none of the original lineup. The release of *Orchestral* (2014) would be Strange's last release, as he died from a heart attack in Egypt in 2015, while Ure would go on to have a string of hits with Ultravox. Visage was in many ways a training ground for Ure and others, as along with the stylistic elements they employed, they represented the new wave, a new romantic sound that is still as influential as it was over forty years ago.

## FEEL THE RAIN LIKE AN
## ENGLISH SUMMER: *VISAGE* (1979)

Plasketes (2013) describes the debut album as 'cultural artefacts that capture the popular imagination especially well. As a first impression, the debut album may take on a mythical status, whether the artist or group achieves enduring success or in rare cases when an initial record turns out to be an apogee for an artist.'[9] Debut albums represent moments of a time in which, collectively, a number of people can capture parts of the populist zeitgeist. A debut album represents many things, either a summation of years of work and development, or a hurried cross-combination of ideas, ideals, and half-baked thoughts. It's a significant milestone as it also has to prove to the record label that the act they have signed will pay off. Further to this, it's a callsign and a statement of intent, and it can often be hard to follow for some acts, especially if it propels the act directly into the mainstream and public consciousness. It's an integral stage, one that often cuts a path for the artist and their future direction. Visage's debut album is more of a demonstration of collaborative ideas, a test bed and a hint of things to come, yet for many, *The Anvil* (1982), although not as commercially successful, would be more musically in tune and consistent with both itself and the albums released during that year.

The cover of *Visage*, designed by the band and illustrated by Iain Gillies, shows two dancers, mid-pose, in front of a silhouetted band. In an open interpretation, it feels like it does indeed see the new guard replacing the old, and even though the album heavily features traditional instruments, it perhaps now time for these musical entities to move on. Co-produced, recorded, and mixed by Martin Rushent between 1979 and 1980 at Genetic Studios in Reading, Berkshire, the album is essentially a combination of Ure's production skills. The session players skillfully interplay between instruments and electronics and Strange's vision, a mix between cabaret, futuristic, and the cryptic.

The album's opening track, 'Visage,' is daring, optimistic, and full of hope. Musically, it's full of opulent ideas, and as pointed out previously, it sets down the path (contextually) of the remainder of the album. This is bookended by the lyrics, which bookmark a sense of oncoming change, as the lyrics of 'Stranger' point toward:

New styles, new shapes,
New modes, that's the role my passion takes,
Oh my visage.

Sonically, it begins quite traditionally: a piano motif on top of a 4/4 beat, interrupted by European influences; electronic percussion, elements of Kraftwerk and/or krautrock. However, it is new wave and Post-Punk straight off. Adamson's bass and Egan's drums serve as a template for the aforementioned genre's rhythmic unit.

This is augmented by a lead synthesised line that lifts and elevates. Strange's vocal presentation makes use of Bowie's euphoric vocal choruses, certainly a homage to his idol and now cultural collaborator. At two minutes, we enter a completely different zone, one much akin to Giorgio Morroder, 4/4 kick drum and arpeggiated electronic bass. It has the same sonic exploration and futurism as Bowie's *Heroes* (1977), yet the amount of musical breakdowns, particularly at the beginning, somewhat stuns the momentum of the track. However, this is made up toward the end as a sense of climax returns, making up for lost time. A fast-paced arpeggiated sequence links between this and 'Blocks and Blocks.' Here, the link between Magazine and Visage are clear. Both Adamson (bass) and Egan (drums) provide a solid back beat. What becomes established early and is perhaps overused is electronic percussion (snares) washed through long reverb effects; while attention grabbing, it is perhaps distracting at times. Synthesised strings lead the chorus, augmenting Strange's lyrics, which are difficult to penetrate. Again, breaks are used, and in this case, a middle section is filled with an array of electronic sounds. The track ends with a guitar solo by McGough that sounds like a last-minute overdub.

There is a sense of melancholy, a reflective quality in Strange's lyrics. If the essence of the New Romantics' sound was escapism, an optimistic view on the world (as per 'Visage') is odd. As Reynolds (2005) points out, 'For all its brisk electro disco rhythms, Visage's music was sepia-toned and at times almost funeral, with Strange's vocals exuding a fey sadness' (2005, 326). 'The Dancer,' the album's first instrumental, is a truly odd addition. It begins as a traditional rock song, with a distorted guitar providing the main lead. Ultimately, it is a piece produced by Ure and a demonstration of his developing his production skills in the studio.

This could be the soundtrack for the Blitz and was perhaps played back at either Billy's or the Blitz. Indeed, Rushnet first heard Visage's mixes at Billy's, and this would be pivotal for other labels to get a taste of the act, including Polydor, whom they signed in 1980. Ure was acutely aware of the value of the clubs, and to a lesser degree, Strange's contributions to the group, commenting:

> He was a blank canvas, him and his connections and, I suppose, the buzz that was coming out of the end of Billy's and the beginning of the Blitz. That whole thing was invaluable. That was his contribution. He didn't write the lyrics and he wasn't really a great singer. I had to sing the songs first and then pump my voice into his ear, and what came out of his mouth was a close enough representation. His value was the face, the connections, the make-up artists, the clothes, the style, the look—all of that stuff was just as important. So there was no question of me doing this as a vehicle for myself. (Ure, quoted in Jones 2020, 181)

Ure's ambition was twofold: professional development and the attention and label support he needed to take Ultravox into the charts. 'Tar,' first released on Radar Records in November 1979, was the first single, and a rerecorded version appears here on the album. The difference between them is both pitch, as the 7-inch version is lower and the timing differences on the LP version are slightly faster, along the obvious production values that Rushnet brought to the table. Part infomercial, part futuristic, it's an interesting addition to the LP. It is perhaps the closest track on the album that resembles the sound of Japan's Yellow Magic Orchestra (YMO). Their self-titled album, released in 1978, featured the single 'Firecracker,' which was an international success.

YMO marked a more upbeat and positive sound, using electronic devices as opposed to the sound of the cold and distant European acts. Next, the album takes a U-turn, into a place of epic creation and to a track that would go on to define the careers of all the band members.

Strange laments in 'Fade to Grey' with: 'Feel the rain like an English summer.' These lyrics clearly define the melancholy and magic the group, along with Strange, captured with this track, and as of September 2022, the current total streamed plays on Spotify of 'Fade to Grey' was 53,135,913,[10] obviously displaying the track's long-encompassing inspiration and admiration. The background of the song is washed with as much mystique as the atmosphere of the song itself. Released as the second single from the LP in November 1980, it began its life as an instrumental, developed and co-written by Payne and Currie, and Ure, who carried out much of its production, could hear its potential upon first listen, as he recalls:

> It was a lovely instrumental piece when I first heard it. Billy was touring with Gary Numan's Tubeway Army and he and the other keyboard player Chris used to jam this little piece of music at soundchecks. They recorded it when they finished the tour and they played me the piece of music and I just fell in love with it—I thought it was fantastic. So I wrote the lyrics and the top line melody to *Fade to Grey* and turned it into a Visage song.[11]

Its palatial opening, as a drifting synthesised string sound begins, is closely followed by what sounds like an electronic pulse, more than likely generated so the other members of the band could keep time with the synthesised bass line. A drum machine accompanies this bass line, which follows the phrase, 'Devenir gris,' wistfully sung by Egan's girlfriend at the time, Brigitte Arens. It's icy, cold, and already sounds like a future classic.

Part of its originality is the seamless flow between electronics and instruments, much of which is thanks to Cedric Sharpley's metronomic and soulful drumming. Lyrically, it's melancholic and reflective:

One man on a lonely platform,
One case sitting by his side,
Two eyes staring cold and silent,
Show fear as he turns to hide.

It's filled with a romantic classicism and sound symphonic, as it is the only track on the album that seems orchestrated, and as discussed at the beginning of this chapter, it has a 'dandyist' atmosphere. This was personified in the video for 'Fade to Grey,' which featured Strange and friend Julia Fodor. It was the first video to be directed by Godley and Creme (10cc), who would go on to define the music video in the 1980s, directing for Duran Duran and the Police. It places Strange in a kabuki style (Japanese dance-drama) dress as Fodor mimics the French lyrics. The video would be another reason for the popularity of the song, particularly in Germany and Switzerland. The would become the New Romantics' anthem, and it is still widely influential, so much so that Strange would go on to release an orchestrated version of the track in 2014 as part of the 'Fade to Grey' orchestral suite.

While Ure and others can indeed be credited as producers and co-writers, it is important to acknowledge Strange's contribution here of aesthetics, style, and presentation, all of which determined his success and legacy. The popularity of the song had taken Strange and the band by surprise, and it sparked a rivalry within the scene, with Strange suggesting:

> Visage had grown beyond anyone's wildest expectations. Fade to Grey had been a hit and we had stolen a march on the rest of the New Romantic Scene, getting our debut album out long before Spandau Ballet released theirs. There was always an element of friendly rivalry between us. We didn't mind the others doing well, as long as we did better. (Strange 2002, 68)

'Malpaso Man' follows, and the album returns to its powerhouse sound: loud drums and wailing guitars. An arpeggiated pulse accompanies Strange's vocoded vocals, and like many other tracks on the album, it is part art rock, part Post-Punk. What it does have is a broad sound design; apart from the traditional instruments, it is populated with an array of sounds and vocal samples that help populate the sound stage.

Along with this, synthesised trumped elements allow for it to have an almost regal and triumphant sound. Malpaso (translated from Spanish to 'badstep' or 'slipup') mostly is a homage to Clint Eastwood, it seems, as the lyrics suggest:

Small cheroot, black hat, cold eyes,
(Malpaso man),
Pointed boots, no heart, never cries,
(Malpaso man).

The album seems to sway between powerhouse, production lead (via both Rushnet and Ure) and that of fully fledged and well-conceived tracks. This is the case with 'Mind of a Toy,' the third single release from the album, released in March 1981. A drum machine and a synthesizer lead the way during its introduction, before a familiar drum and bass rhythm take charge. What's striking is the juxtaposition of these worlds; the introduction is melancholic and distant, and this is then interrupted by a more forward motion verse. This motif becomes part of the overall language of the album. Yet, what comes in the midsection, a reintroduction of the intro, is perhaps the most well-crafted section on the album: a combination of duelling chime-like synthesisers, interspersed by recordings made in a children's playground. The track ends with distant music boxes that spill and fall into the next production. Again, the single did well, peaking at number thirteen in March 1981.[12] This was aided no doubt by another video produced by Godley and Creme that featured Strange as a Little Lord Fauntleroy, a giant child's toy house, and Strange being pulled around like a puppet.

'Moon over Moscow' follows, which takes a cross-section of influences and assembles them together; Giorgio Moroder, Sparks most notably, Yellow Magic Orchestra. An instrumental, its title suggests its theme, that of escapism. The production levels are high, and it is obvious that Ure here is in the driving seat, testing out and experimenting with the studio. Like the other instrumentals on the album, they are stark contrasts to what the other more fully developed productions provide. 'Visa-Age' brings the more complete sound into focus again. An interesting mix between Post-Punk and proto disco, it also leans heavily on Numan's sound: that of the electric and electronic working in harmony. Science fiction and futurism, themes previously explored, return here to the fold, yet the lyrics are uninspiring, perhaps rushed, as Strange sings:

Visa-age,
(I know the place),

Visa-age,
(I can't forget).

There is not much more to say about tracks such as 'Visa-Age' as they
represent moments in time in the studio environment, demonstrations
of musicians' ability. However, the song does contain some interesting
sound effects: a lone whistler, falling rain, and the sound of a passing train
that is perhaps a homage to Kraftwerk's Trans Europe Express. The album
ends with the wonderfully apocalyptic 'The Steps.' It's both eerie and
frightening, almost like the sound design of a cheap horror soundtrack,
then fanfared synthesisers fill the space.

Musically, no doubt, again heavily influenced by the B side of Bowie's
*Low* (1977), it is a truly epic track to place at the end of the album due to
its atmospherics, as it, like many others, sits so starkly against the rest of
the productions. *Visage* represents the most commercially successful debut
album documented in this book. Commercially, it would go gold in both
France and Germany.[13] Critically, it would be less well received, as Mike
Nicholls from *Record Mirror* from November 1980 suggests:

> I wouldn't go as far as to say that Visage are amongst the new masters
> of rock–they are decorative and they have too many of their own
> commitments anyway. But this is a highly listenable album of quality
> background music.[14]

## TECHNOLOGY

Music sampling instruments have come a long way and can be traced back
to the American inventor Harry Chamberlin. Produced between 1949 and
1956, the 'Chamberlin' was a traditional keyboard instrument, with a revolutionary difference. Underneath each key was a tape machine mechanism
that played prerecorded loops when the key was depressed. The tape head
was then amplified and passed through a loudspeaker, and although each
tape loop was only a few seconds long, it meant you could have an entire
orchestra at your fingertips. In the early 1960s, his business partner and
salesman Bill Franson had a number of disagreements with Chamberlin, and
soon Franson shipped a number of units across the pond.

The Chamberlin then became the 'Franson,' and eventually, via
Norman and Les Bradley's Bradmatic LTD, the 'Mellotron Mark I.' It
would not be until the mid- to late 1960s that the Mellotron would enter

into popular musicmaking via multi-instrumentalist Graham Bond, and most notably, in 1966, on the Beatles' 'Strawberry Fields Forever.' The sampler would go digital on the banks of the Thames, London, in 1969, with the help of British inventor and EMS (Electronic Music Studios) owner Peter Zinovieff. Along with David Cocherell and software engineer Peter Gronogo, the EMS Musys System ran on two PDP-8 computers. Cumbersome and expensive, it failed to achieve commercial success, and it would not be until 1979 that the first polyphonic digital sampler would become commercially available.

The Fairlight, developed by Peter Vogel and Kim Rykie in Australia, would change the face of musicmaking in the 1980s, as it was not only a computer but a digital audio workstation. It featured a lightpen that could input commands directly into the computer itself. In 1979, Vogel demonstrated it to Peter Gabriel, who was making *Peter Gabriel* (1980) at the time, and he was so overwhelmed with the instrument, he offered to become a UK sales representative to promote it. At 12,000 pounds, it would only be sold to rock's royalty at the time, which included John Paul Jones (Led Zeppelin) and Rick Wright (Pink Floyd). Egan, in *Electronic Sound Maker Magazine* from August 1984, discussed some of the technological assistance used on the production of *Visage*, which included the Fairlight CMI:

> We used *everything* on that album. We had a GS2, two Yamaha grands, two ARP Odysseys, about three Yamaha string synths, a CS80 and a Minimoog. We used a Fairlight on that album, we had the first one that came over from Australia.[15]

As the drummer, Egan often had to play along with electronic percussion generated by drum machines, which was no mean feat in the late 1970s, as Egan expands:

> I was using a Roland CR78 drum machine. This was before the TR808 came out remember. Of course in those days it was difficult to get everything in sync—life before the Linn drum![16]

Egan also used Simmons Drums on the production of *Visage*. Used as a replacement for traditional drums, Dave Simmons developed the SDS-3, 4, and SDS-8 in 1979 while working at an St.Albans company called Musicaid. The SDS-V would become a very popular drum kit in the 1980s, where each drum head was connected to a 'drum brain' or part-synthesizer that would trigger the synthetic sound. As a keen technologist, Egan soon was introduced, commenting:

The drums didn't present any problems because just before the start of recording *Visage*, Richard Burgess had introduced me to Simmons percussion. I remember him showing me this piece of board, which turned out to be the SDS4, I think. It wasn't properly finished at that time—it was just a board with some wires hanging off it and the numbers 1-4 printed on it. I asked Richard what they were and he said "they're the outputs", so we plugged them in, used a Roland Microcomposer to clock everything, and every time I wanted to change one of the sounds I had to get a little screwdriver out and adjust the pots.[17]

The Roland Microcomposer would be key to the production of *Visage* as it was used by Rushnett to keep the electronic instruments in time and allowing the user to use many instances of the pitch CVs to a single Gate channel, which could create polyphonic parts. Rushent used the Microcomposer in a similar fashion when working with the Human League, effectively to keep synchronisation:

The timecode is generated by the MC8, the Roland Microcomposer. If the song is 180 bars long, we feed in '180'. If there's any 2/4 or 3/4 bars, they get written in as well. So on the tape we now have the time-code, and from that we can run the Microcomposer which will drive the synthesisers, and we can run the Linn drum machine.[18]

In many ways, the Roland's Microcomposer became an additional player, as what could be done by the keyboard player could now be done by a machine, as Rushent explains:

The MC8 really replaces the keyboard, it sends out exactly the signals the keyboard would send out if you were playing it. There are three parameters that are important to a synthesiser in terms of the signal that it gets from the keyboard. In fact on some synths there are more than that, but the basic three are: control voltage, which denotes the pitch of the note; the gate, or trigger pulse, which denotes how long the note's going to sound for, coupled with the ADSR which will give you attack, decay and so on; and step time, which denotes the length of time that the note occupies—it may not *sound* for that long, but it's a crotchet, say, and that's its value. The control voltage is very simple, you just program in all the notes in sequence that you want. Gate time then denotes how long you want each to last.[19]

Ure saw technology as an extension of what he could already do, and it was perhaps this parallel between the past and the future that made Visage sound more current at the time. Ure certainly saw this as a building block for the formation of the band. Perhaps this is what such machines brought about. In all, Egan, Ure, Rushent, and Formula used technology as a collaborative partner, domesticating cutting-edge technology, a story and process that is still evident in the sound of today's electronic music production.

## CONCLUSION

The different spheres in which electronic music production exists today is overwhelming, and 'much of the difficulty in talking about electronic-music aesthetics lies in identifying what electronic music is and deciding whether it is too big to discuss as one entity' (Demers 2010, 135). Electronic music today is very much about placing its production style in a genre, a classification as a tool for marketing or so Apple Music or Spotify can classify an act and playlist them to potential streamers and listeners. Frow explains that genres are all about the communication of knowledge, in that 'genre, we might say, is a set of conventional and highly organised constraints on the production and interpretation of meaning' (Frow 2005, 10). Visage took genre and split it across cultural, technological, and fashion-based ideologies, and indeed, its revolving scenes. For Strange and Egan, it was the club scene in London; for Ure and the other musicians, it was about not only an exploration of technology and the studio, but an exploitation of that space, not only as a creative exercise, but also as a means to make financial reward.

One could say that Visage was made to make hits, to trial and error how music(s) could break into the mainstream, which they both did, to levels of which they could have only dreamed. However, as Visage did not function as a normal band, they, more than any other act, depended on their equipment more than anything else, as it was the apparatus through which success would come. Even though their sound was only partly electronic, the work that Ure and others made during the production of *Visage* continues to inform the sound of today, a sound in which musicians interact with technology, an arena where musicians, much the same as the members of Visage, are still open to suggestion.

## NOTES

1. A. Bennett (2017), Wrapped in stardust: glam rock and the rise of David Bowie as pop entrepreneur, *Continuum*, 31:4, 574–82, DOI: 10.1080/10304312.2017.1334371 (accessed March 12, 2022).

2. See also https://www.theguardian.com/music/musicblog/2016/jan/15/david-bowie-starman-top-of-the-pops (accessed September 8, 2022).

3. Ibid.

4. See also https://www.anothermanmag.com/life-culture/10164/the-song-that-shot-roxy-music-to-stardom (accessed September 8, 2022).

5. See also https://dangerousminds.net/comments/steve_strange_chrissie_hynde_offend_all_of_england_as_punk_band (accessed March 21, 2022).

6. See also https://shapersofthe80s.com/2015/11/09/%e2%9e%a4-princess-julia-relives-the-day-when-1980-went-boom/ (accessed May 6, 2022).

7. See also https://www.classicpopmag.com/2022/08/midge-ure-interview/ (accessed September 6, 2021).

8. See also https://recordcollectormag.com/articles/days-ure (accessed March 8, 2022).

9. See also https://www.researchgate.net/publication/290804434_Please_allow_me_to_introduce_myself_Essays_on_debut_albums (accessed April 11, 2022).

10. Streaming data available at: https://open.spotify.com/album/6NsHH43MNyI3q6Uv53jSDf (accessed September 14, 2002).

11. See also https://www.henleystandard.co.uk/news/music/114165/we-ll-have-a-grey-old-time-pledges-synthpop-pioneer.html (accessed September 12, 2022).

12. See also https://www.officialcharts.com/search/singles/mind%20of%20a%20toy/ (accessed August 2, 2022).

13. See also https://infodisc.fr/Chanson_Certifications.php (accessed September 15, 2022).

14. See also https://worldradiohistory.com/UK/Record-Mirror/80s/81/Record-Mirror-1981-02-21-OCR.pdf (accessed September 19, 2022).

15. See also http://www.muzines.co.uk/articles/searching-for-the-perfect-beat/3385 (accessed September 21, 2022).

16. See also http://www.muzines.co.uk/articles/behind-visage/7949 (accessed September 21, 2022).

17. See also http://www.muzines.co.uk/articles/human-league-in-the-studio/4246 (accessed September 21, 2022).

18. Ibid.

19. See also https://www.soundonsound.com/people/martin-rushent-producer (accessed July 20, 2022).

# 11

## CONCLUSION

## Influence and Afterword

Electronic musical instrument technology evolves with each passing decade. At the dawn of the 1980s, the analogue synthesisers discussed in this book—the MiniMoog, for example—were in line for slaughter, as MIDI and digital platforms would soon replace them. Analogue synthesizers and their associated workflows have not only survived numerous evolutions, but they have also regained a somewhat mythological status. Over the last decade, as CPU and RAM-processing power has become faster and cheaper to implement, this status has been turned into a very direct and profitable selling point by brands such as Arturia, which have developed VST (Virtual Studio Technology) plugin versions of many of the synthesizer brands and models. What can only be termed as 'boutique' processes and effects in contemporary electronic music production are becoming more and more incorporated into virtual synthesizers, and such developments and trends have largely been, as Toffler (1980) suggests, 'informed, supplemented and aided by pro audio marketing, where both the professional and consumer merge as "the prosumer"' (Toffler 1980, 101).

Current electronic music producers now very much rely on emulations of analogue synthesisers, as the originals are very much out of reach financially, so the field position, economic class, and habits within current electronic musicmaking reveals a vigorous battle between the so-called prosumer by considering a new socio-historic subject (the prosumer) and the space of production (the project studio).

Cole (2011) defines this as:

> The project studio and prosumer reconfigure some, but not all, of the dominant relations within the wider social or economic field. Thus, we can see that although prosumers are not economically determined, their

relative autonomy is itself directly tied to changes in the structure of social production and consumption (Cole 2011, 458).

If we consider Gary Numan, who had access to instruments like the MiniMoog, and more cottage or industrious bands like Throbbing Gristle, who built a lot of their own devices, the ideal of cultural 'capital' comes into focus. Pierre Bourdieu's *Distinction: A Social Critique of the Judgement of Taste* (1984) considers different forms of 'capital' in terms of 'economic, cultural, social and symbolic relationships, referring to the fact that they are all utilised by members of the social field in order to attempt dominance for their judgements' (Bourdieu 1984, 1). Bourdieu also points toward what he referred to as 'social assets' (in arts and education) that allow for social mobility beyond economic means.

These, it seems, are most likely to determine what constitutes taste in cultural fashion. This, in turn, allows it to become a form of cultural capital, in that:

> There is an economy of cultural goods, but it has a specific logic. Sociology endeavours to establish the conditions in which the consumers of cultural goods, and their taste for them, are produced, and at the same time to describe the different ways of appropriating such of these objects as are regarded at a particular moment as works of art, and the social conditions of the constitution of the mode of appropriation that is considered legitimate. But one cannot fully understand cultural practices unless 'culture', in the restricted, normative sense of ordinary usage, is brought back into 'culture' in the anthropological sense, and the elaborated taste for the most refined objects is reconnected with the elementary taste for the flavours of food (Ibid., 1).

If we consider Bourdieu theory more closely, we can see that social and, indeed, geographical issues perhaps conditioned the users of these machines, be it Sheffield or London, into using brands based on this. There is another interesting note to this that relies on the knowledge base of the user, as both Chris Carter and Chris Watson were electronics hobbyists and had an understanding of not only their instruments, but also of the technology and circuitry behind it, whereas Gary Numan and Daniel Miller did not possess these skills.

Gaining such knowledge did and does not immediately make you a better performer and composer, but perhaps had its advantages. As Zagorski-Thomas (2014) suggests, expanding further on Bourdieu's notion of 'capital,' it could be linked with a person's social and cultural 'position,' commenting:

> On an economic level, the spending power of an audience and its abil-
> ity to buy the output and thereby confer value on it is one fundamental
> use of capital. On the other hand, cultural capital relates to the tacit and
> explicit knowledge that confers power to an individual; social capital
> relates to power that stems from a person's position within some social
> grouping and symbolic power relates to ideas such as prestige and hon-
> our. (Zagorski-Thomas 2014, 131)

As both Carter and Watson never made it to *Top of the Pops*, Numan
was in a dominant position of cultural capital, in that his label, Beggars,
was in a position to provide more social positioning and prestige. It is
possible this dystopian sound was informed by those who have cultural
capital, well-known producers for example, who in turn 'inform the
practises of a cohort of mastering engineers who admire those in question
or the individual's work, mediated by the social field, which affects a part
of the cultural domain' (Ibid., 131). For today's producers of electronic
music, many machines discussed in this book are far beyond the reach of
many, a similar factor also during 1977–1980.

However, what has changed is computational technology. Thanks
to companies like Arturia, modern electronic music producers now have
access to digital plugins, or VST (Virtual Studio Technology) versions of the
MiniMoog, Roland 606, System 100, and EMS Synthi, and for many, this
is where the great debate on the use of electronic musicmaking, of whether
using hardware or software for production begins. Kaiser (2017) attempts
to define the relationship between capital and the user's relationship with
technology, and he argues there are many aspects of analogue software that
cannot be emulated by software plugins, suggesting that:

> The credibility gap of software emulation in music production com-
> prises tentative, olfactory and gustatory sensations, process-oriented
> aspects of workflow, as well as aspects of a hardware's physical charac-
> teristics, and time-dependent aspects. (Kaiser 2019, 3)

Many of the musicians or nonmusicians documented in this book had
no real formal musical training; they learned to play their synthesisers
and electronics of choice via interacting with physical hardware, in that
the physicality of turning knobs to make sonic adjustments and proce-
dural processes, changing tape or waiting for valves in amplifiers to heat
up. Such processes can help us define some of the aesthetic differences
between using hardware and software devices, and here the role of ergonomics helps clarify the relationship between the musician and the job at

hand. It focuses on the design of work areas or work tasks to improve job performance and the ergonomics of each process, both physical and virtual.

Both approaches are broadly defined as follows:

- Physical Processing: the tactile and hands-on process of using faders and knobs to adjust parameters to make electronic music.
- Virtual Processing: the non-tactile process of using a mouse or a touchscreen to adjust parameters to make electronic music.

While virtual processes can make workflow more streamlined (via automation and digital recall), electronic musicmakers of today generally use an ergonomically hybrid approach, via the use of both physical and virtual musicmaking tools. In the end, 'cultural capital' is not just about simply buying or accumulating technology; it's about people having access to technology, or more so, processes that would usually be unavailable to them.

Free multitrack electronic music production platforms like 'Reaper,' which offer a suite of free VST, composed in a very smartly designed program, have had a huge and profound impact on the electronic music production industry. In order to differentiate themselves, companies like Arturia lean heavily on taglines like 'authentic,' 'warm,' and 'vintage' to help market and sell their virtual synthesizers. One of the possible contributing factors to this is the collective consideration that these analogue technologies and processes of the past provide a more distinctive sound, and standing out 'sonically' from the crowd becomes more and more important.

One fundamental separation between both physical and virtual electronic musicmaking still exists: the role of human objectivity. As much as virtual synthesizer plugins can offer, a plugin preset cannot make experienced and informed musical decisions on the fly or offer years of tried and tested methodologies made by the likes of Carter, Watson, Numan, Miller et al. Any musician knows that a new plugin or piece of hardware can bring about new possibilities, but that it can, at the same time, bring about limitations. Perhaps these levels of human objectivity are at an end, as Birchnell (2018) suggests, 'in some instances, technologies are the root cause of human obsolescence and drive redundancies in occupations, skills and livelihoods' (Birchnell 2018, 22).

The use of artificial intelligence and machine learning in current electronic musicmaking brings many considerations. Algorithmic control of what has primarily been a human-driven enterprise will see the domain drastically shift over the next decade. Stern and Razlogova (2019) suggest AI and machine learning 'devalues the people's aesthetic labour as it establishes higher standards for recordings online.'[1] Nonetheless, it is important to recognize that perhaps AI and machine learning are just variants of traditional electronic musicmaking in that far from the spectacular rhetoric around AI as an emergent form of nonhuman agency, we find a very familiar set of agencies—financial, corporate, technical, musical, and human—hard at work in a new setting. Emergent technologies have led to the development of extended electronic and industrial musicmaking over the last number of years, and these technologies have played a role in shaping the sounds of today and of tomorrow.

AI and machine learning will undoubtedly change the way in which the electronic music of the future will be produced, and going forward, electronic musicians will have to fight and strive toward keeping it a human-centred process, and if required, incorporate algorithmic approaches that include collaboration with humans rather than attempting to replace or outsell them.

Many of the acts discussed in this book relied and utilised an operational language, control voltage, which allowed synthesisers, sequencers, and drum machines to communicate with each other. However, due to the lack of standardisation, each manufacturer essentially had to develop their own protocol, which included CV/Gate and Digital Control Bus (DCB), as ulatized by Roland. CV/Gate was the more common option on many devices throughout the late 1970s; it works primarily by the voltage controlling the pitch and the gate controlling the note on/off functionality. Much of what this process uses is essentially what the modular systems built by Moog in the late 1960s implemented; a patch cord could interconnect each module. Thus, the control voltage would allow a synthesiser and drum machine to communicate with one another while the gate function simply communicated when the signal went high and to turn off when the signal went low. Chris Carter of Throbbing Gristle would have used this process extensively on *20 Jazz Funk Greats* to allow his Roland 808 to communicate with this modular synthesizer. Control Voltage was an extremely expressive functionality that allowed new electronic groups to have a much more synchronised sound. However, due to the instability of analogue machines, it was never quite as reliable as it should have been.

Roland first considered a new approach, and in 1981 its president, Ikutaro Kakehashi, proposed to an American manufacturer, Oberheim Electronics, the development of a universal protocol for synthesisers to use. The involvement of Oberheim brought about a more complicated and costly process, which led Kakehashi to Sequential Circuits and Dave Smith, and in October 1982, Musical Instrument Digital Interface (MIDI) was developed and implemented by Roland, Yamaha, Korg, Kawai, and Sequential Circuits. MIDI, unlike CV/Gate, does not use audio signals to communicate information. Instead, a MIDI cable can carry up to sixteen channels of information, including pitch and volume. Still in use today, its most common function is to send pitch information from a MIDI keyboard to a VST (virtual synthesizer) in an application like Abelton Live. Due to its ease of use, levels of manipulation, and small file size, it is now the dominant communication language for electronic music producers.

It is not the objective of this book to go into great technical detail. However, the implications of the advent of MIDI during the early 1980s had a near-monumental effect on the resulting sound of the decade. Once the MIDI information is recorded in a digital sequencer or computer, it can be played back, and it is perfectly in time as it has been quantized.[2]

While this process indeed made electronic musicmaking and its workflow much easier, it produced a more regulated and conservative music(s), and as a result, the majority of electronic music today somewhat lacks the experimental nature and technological unpredictability of what acts like Throbbing Gristle and Cabaret Voltaire achieved during the late 1970s. So as technological advances came via the microchip and processor, so, too, did a change and/or an alteration of the timbre and experimental nature of synthesised and electronic music produced in Britain.

The acts documented in *Dark Waves* created little sense of community, yet at the same time, they embodied the cultural, social, and economic climate of Britain in the 1970s. For them, the dystopian sound of Britain was the ambition to express and communicate subject matter and content not yet addressed in popular musicmaking. As technology would dominate much of this music(s) progression in the 1980s, the legacy of the acts in *Dark Waves* blurs the borders between noise and music, as much of their work would go on to inspire the coming decades and much of the context of this would inform its progression, practises, and history. All this was placed in dystopian times as the Cold War struggled on until 1991, and it was as this ended that a new global economy was born. At this stage, as Reed (2013) suggests:

> The genre's widespread momentary popularity peaked at that premillennial moment of eclipse, but since the dreamed-of future became the past, industrial music hasn't changed its time much, which is why it can see past in the twenty-first century. (Reed 2013, 315)

From their earliest inceptions, the acts made propositions and acts of nonconformity through modern means, and as times changed, so did the machines facilitating this. On a musicological level, the area of musicmaking, documented in this book, has little academic profile. The approaches of the background of the artists documented, along with their use of technology, all happened in the midst and correlations between Punk, Post-Punk, DIY, and electronic music in 1970s Britain.

Frith (2017) identifies music as a special type of aesthetic product because it 'cultivates a sense of community while facilitating transcendence of community' (Frith 2017, 73), and as many of the albums reviewed in this book were recorded and produced in London, through this, there is a sense of awareness that what they created was based on their experience of living during that period in Britain. Many of the acts reviewed were influenced by major art movements (Surrealism, Dadaism), and to a lesser degree, science fiction; thus what they produced was defined by the art they consumed. From this, an inherent sense of experimentalism was born, and as Demers (2019) points out, 'experientialism occurs in any attempt to experiment, to take risks, to do the unexpected. As such, experimentalism can occur anywhere, in any economic class or social situation, and with any type of technology' (2019, 141). Elements of the dystopian sound of remain in contemporary electronic music, and as Fisher (2006) points out, while on first listening to London's Burial:

> Near future, maybe... But listening to *Burial* as I walk through damp and drizzly South London streets in this abortive Spring, it strikes me that the LP is very London Now—which is to say, it suggests a city haunted not only by the past but by lost futures. It seems to have less to do with a near future than with the tantalising ache of a future just out of reach.[3]

Acts like Belbury Poly and Pye Audio Corner tap into these 'lost futures' and reference a hauntological sound world that fully makes use of a sense of place, and much of their productions channel public service advertisements and supernatural stories from television like Children of the Stone (1976) and the Owl Service (1970). However, as Fisher points out, besides the above acts' adaptation of retrofuturism, innovation seems to have been misplaced and/or lost, in that, as Fisher (2012) elaborates:

> What haunts the digital cul-de-sacs of the twenty-first century is not so much the past as all the lost futures that the twentieth century taught us to anticipate. The futures that have been lost were more than a matter of musical style. More broadly, and more troublingly, the disappear-

ance of the future meant the deterioration of a whole mode of social
imagination: the capacity to conceive of a world radically different from
the one in which we currently live. (Fisher 2012, 16)

*Dark Waves* has considered technologically the synthesiser, not only as a
musical instrument but as a tool that soundtracked a changing time. The
synthesizer's current resurgence brings about new (and old) processes,
reconnecting it to the past, again providing outlets for gesture, feedback,
and physicality in both electronic music compositional and performance
paradigms. Throughout the history of software synthesis, obsolescence
has put hardware devices into the backrooms of studio and research labs.
Further to this, some of the operating systems that run hardware synthesizers often go obsolete, leaving their usage limited.

Key to understanding the role of the synthesizer is its sense of independence from updates and software, in that it allows the machine to become, in
a way, immune to the rapid pace of technology, as most of their architecture
and inbuilt circuits remains fixed and autonomous, unreflective of change.
One cannot help but wonder about the possibilities (or lack thereof) of future
ways of musicmaking that may appear, which will again provide electronic
musicians with the opportunity to exploit technology on such a physical level,
or indeed, if the listener can again be so closely aware of sound and its production mechanisms. Ultimately, *Dark Waves* presented the synthesizer, and in
some degree the acts discussed within, as immune from technological retirement and significance, allowing both to remain seminal within the histories of
popular electronic musicmaking both now and into the future.

## NOTES

1. See also J. Sterne and E. Razlogova, Machine Learning in Context, or
Learning from LANDR: Artificial Intelligence and the Platformization of Music Mastering, *Journal of Social Media and Society* Vol. 5, No. 2. https://doi.
org/10.1177/2056305119847525 (accessed March 11, 2022).

2. Quantization (via MIDI) positions data on the nearest grid position that is
musically relevant and is largely designed to correct errors. It can also be used in
a creative way, like altering the rhythmic timing of MIDI data (swing).

3. See also http://k-punk.abstractdynamics.org/archives/007666.html (accessed
September 6, 2022).

# BIBLIOGRAPHY

Aaronovitch, Sam. 1981. *The Road from Thatcherism: The Alternative Economic Strategy*. London: Lawrence & Wishart.

Allen, Robert C. 2011. *Global Economic History: A Very Short Introduction*. Oxford: Oxford University Press.

Amis, M. 1992. "Hard Shoulder," *New Review*, 10 October.

Attali, Jacques. 1977. *Noise: The Political Economy of Music*. Paris: Presses Universitaires de France.

Ball, Hugo. *Dadaist Manifesto*. Read at the first public, Zurich, July 14, 1916.

Ballard, J.G. 1973. *Crash*, 1st ed. London: Picador.

Baxter, J. 2009. *J.G. Ballard's Surrealist Imagination: Spectacular Authorship*. London: Routledge.

Beer, Stafford. 1972. *In the Brain of the Firm*. London: Allen Lane.

Benjamin, Walter, & Rolf Tiedemann. 1999. *The Arcades Project*. Harvard: Belknap Press.

Benn, Tony. 1989. *Against the Tide. Diaries 1973–76*. London: Hutchinson.

Berman, Marshall. 2010. *All That Is Solid Melts into Air*. London: Verso Publishing.

Birrer, Frans A. J. "Definitions and research orientation: do we need a definition of popular music?" in D. Horn, ed., *Popular Music Perspectives* 2 (1985): Gothenburge, Exeter, Ottawa and Reggio Emilia, 99–106.

Birtchnell, T. 2010. "Listening without Ears: Artificial Intelligence in Audio Mastering." *J. Big Data & Society* 4, no. 2, https://doi.org/10.1177/205395171880855.

Bishop, Claire (ed). 2006. *Participation*. Boston: MIT Press.

Black, Lawrence, Hugh Pemberton, & Pat Thane (eds). 2013. *Reassessing Britain*. Manchester: Manchester University Press.

Botstein, Leon. 2001. "Modernism." *Grove Music Online*. Accessed September 30, 2022. https://www.oxfordmusiconline.com/grovemusic/view/10.1093/gmo/9781561592630.001.0001/omo-9781561592630-e-0000040625.

Boulez, Pierre. 1977. *Technology and the Composer*. Times Literary Supplement, May 6.

Bourdieu, Pierre. 1984. *Distinction: A Social Critique of the Judgment of Taste*. Harvard, Cambridge: Harvard University Press.

Bourdieu, Pierre. 2010. *Distinction: A Social Critique of the Judgment of Taste*. Routledge: Abingdon Oxfordshire.

Bowlby, Rachel. "'Half Art': Baudelaire's 'Le Peintre de La Vie Moderne.'" *Daedalus* 143, no. 1 (2014): 46–53. http://www.jstor.org/stable/43297285.

Bracewell, Michael. 2020. *Souvenir*. London: Orion Books.

Brend, Mark. 2012. *The Sound of Tomorrow: How Electronic Music Was Smuggled into the Mainstream*. London: Bloomsbury.

Budd, Alan. 1980. *The Politics of Economic Planning*. London: Fontana, 1978.

Burk, Kathleen, & Alec Cairncross. 1992. *Goodbye, Great Britain: The 1976 IMF Crisis*. Yale: Yale University Press.

Butler, M.J., ed. 2012. *Electronica, Dance and Club Music*. Farnham: Ashgate.

Cascone, Kim. 2000. "Aesthetics of Failure: Post-Digital Tendencies in Contemporary Computer Music." *Computer Music Journal* 24, no. 4, 12–18.

Cohen, Stanley. 1972. *Folk Devils and Moral Panics*. London: Taylor & Francis.

Cole, S.J. 2011. "The Prosumer and the Project Studio: The Battle for Distinction in the Field of Music Recording," *Journal of Sociology* 45, no. 3, 447–63.

Collins, N., M. Schedel, & S. Wilson, eds. 2013. *Electronic Music: Cambridge Introductions to Music*. Cambridge: Cambridge University Press.

Connell, J., & C. Gibson, C. 2013. *SoundTracks: Popular Music Identity and Place*. London: Taylor and Francis.

Cox, Christopher, & Daniel Warner (eds.). 2007. *Audio Culture: Readings in Modern Music Paperback*. London: Continuum.

Crossley, Nick. 2015. *Networks of sound, style and subversion: The punk and post-punk worlds of Manchester, London, Liverpool and Sheffield, 1975–80*. Manchester: Manchester University Press.

CSE London Working Group. *The Alternative Economic Strategy: A Labor Movement Response to the Economic Crisis*. London: CSE Books.

Dafoe, Allen. 2015. On Technological Determinism: A Typology, Scope Conditions, and a Mechanism, *Science, Technology, & Human Values* 40, no. 6, 1047–76.

Daniel, Drew. 2003. *Throbbing Gristle's Twenty Jazz Funk Greats* (33 1/3). London: Continuum.

Debord, Guy. 1994. *The Society of the Spectacle*. Boston: MIT Press.

Deen, R.T. 2009. *The Oxford Handbook of Computer Music*. Oxford: Oxford University Press.

Demers, Joanna. 2010. *Listening Through the Noise: The Aesthetics of Experimental Electronic Music*. Oxford, UK: Oxford University Press.

De Maria, R., C. Heesok, S. Zacher (eds.). 2013. *A Companion to British Literature, Volume 4: Victorian and Twentieth Century*. London: John Wiley & Sons.

Dick, Philip K. 2012. *Flow My Tears, the Policeman Said*. First Mariner books ed. Boston: Mariner Books, Houghton Mifflin Harcourt.

Dick, Philip K. 2010. *Do Androids Dream of Electric Sheep?* 1st ed. Los Angeles: Boom! Studios.

Emmerson, Simon (ed.). 1986. *The Language of Electroacoustic Music*. London: Palgrave Macmillan.

Eno, Brian. 1996. *A Year with Swollen Appendices*. London: Faber & Faber.

Feenberg, Andrew. 1999. *Questing Technology*. London: Routledge.

Fish, Mick. 2002. *Industrial Evolution: Through the Eighties with Cabaret Voltaire*. London: SAF Publishing.

Fisher, Mark. 2016. *The Weird and the Eerie*. London: Repeater Publications.

Fitting, Peter. 1987. "Futurecop: The Neutralization of Revolt in 'Blade Runner'." *Science Fiction Studies* 14, no. 3, 340–54. http://www.jstor.org/stable/4239842.

Forster, E.M. 2011. *The Machine Stops*. London: Penguin Classics.

Frith, Simon, W. Straw, & J. Street (eds.). 2001. *The Cambridge Companion to Pop and Rock*. Cambridge: Cambridge University Press.

Frith, Simon (ed.). 2004. *Popular Music: Critical Concepts in Media and Cultural Studies*. London: Routledge.

Frith, Simon. 2017. *Taking Popular Music Seriously*. London: Routledge.

Frith, Simon, & H. Horne. 1987. *Art Into Pop* (1st ed.). Routledge: London.

Frith, Simon. 1998. *Performing Rites on the Value of Popular Music*. Harvard: Harvard University Press.

Gasiorek, Andrjez. 2005. *J.G. Ballard*. Manchester: Manchester University Press.

Goldberg, R.I. 1979. *Performance Art: From Futurism to the Present*. London: Thames and Hudson.

Goodwin, Andrew. 1992. "Rationalization and democratization in the new technologies of popular music," in *Popular Music and Communication*, Second Edition. London: James Lull.

Hall, Joseph. 1981. *Mundus Alter ET Idem (The World Different and the Same)*. Yale, CT: Yale University Press.

Hebdige, Dick. 1979. *Subculture: The Meaning of Style*. London: Methuen.

Hegarty, Paul. 2007. *Noise Music: A History*. London: Bloomsbury.

Hickson, Kevin. 2005. *The IMF Crisis of 1976 and British Politics: Keynesian Social Democracy, Monetarism and Economic Liberalism: The 1970s Struggle in British Politics*. London: I.B.Tauris.

Holland, Stuart. 1975. *The Socialist Challenge*. London: Quartet Books.

Houk, Deborah. 1997. "Self-Construction and Sexual Identity in Nineteenth-Century French Dandyism." *French Forum* 22, no. 1, 59–73. http://www.jstor.org/stable/40540408.

Huxley, Aldous. 1947. *The Perennial Philosophy*. London: Harper Perennial.

Huxley, Aldous. 2006. *Brave New World*. London: Harper Perennial.

Jones, Dylan. 2021. *Sweet Dreams: The Story of the New Romantics*. London: Faber & Faber.

Jones, Steve. 1992. *Rock Formation: Music, Technology, and Mass Communication*. 3 vols. Foundations of Popular Culture. Thousand Oaks, CA: SAGE Publications, Inc., https://dx.doi.org/10.4135/9781483325491.

Joyce, James. 1990. *Ulysses*. London: Vintage Press.

Keane, David. 1981. *The Quest for "Musically Interesting" Structures in Computer Music*, International Computer Music Conference, 3–18.

Knapp, Bettina L. 1980. *Antonin Artaud Man of Vision*. Cleveland: Ohio University Press.

Kunz, W.M. 2006. *Culture Conglomerates: Consolidation in the Motion Picture and Television Industries*. London: Rowman & Littlefield.

Lay, Paul. 2007. "Reading Camus in Salford—*Steeped in European culture, Ian Curtis epitomized the 1970s young British working-class intellectual*," *Prospect*, November 25, accessed July 12, 2022. https://www.prospectmagazine.co.uk/magazine/readingcamusinsalford.

Leydon, R. 2004. "Forbidden Planet: Effects and Affects in the Electro-Avant-Garde," in *Off the Planet: Music, Sound and Science Fiction Cinema*, edited by P. Hayward. London: John Libbey.

Longhurst, Brian, & Danijela Bogdanovic. 2014. *Popular Music and Society*, 3rd edition. Hoboken, NJ: Wiley Publishing.

Low, Setha, & Neil Smith. 2006. *The Politics of Public Space*. London: Routledge.

Maconie, Stewart. 2005. *Cider with Roadies*. London: Ebury.

Marcuse, H. 1964. *One-Dimensional Man*. Boston: Beacon Press.

Martinetti, F.T. 1973. In U. Appolonio, ed., *Futurist Manifestos*. London: Thames and Hudson.

Marx, L. 2011. "Technology: The Emergence of a Hazardous Concept." *Social Research* 64, no. 3.

Mayr, Erasmus. 2011. *Understanding Human Agency*. Oxford University Press, Oxford.

McLuhan, Marshall. 1967. *The Medium Is the Message*, 9th ed. Berkeley: Gingko Press.

Merton, Robert. 2018. *Social Science Quotations: Who Said What, When, and Where*. London: Routledge.

Middleton, Richard. 1990. *Studying Popular Music*. London, McGraw-Hill Education.

Morra, Irene. 2013. *Britishness, Popular Music, and National Identity: The Making of Modern Britain* (1st ed.). London: Routledge. https://doi.org/10.4324/9780203503218.

Moylan, T. 2002. *Scraps of the Untainted Sky: Science Fiction, Utopia, Dystopia*. Boulder: Westview-Perseus Press.

Numan, Gary. 2020. *(R)evolution: The Autobiography*. London: Constable.

Ogburn, W.F. 1947. "How Technology Changes Society." *The ANNALS of the American Academy of Political and Social Science* 249, no. 1, 81–88. https://doi.org/10.1177/000271624724900111.

Ogburn, W.F. 1964. *Culture and Social Change: Selected Papers*. Chicago: Chicago University Press.

Orwell, George. 1949. *Nineteen Eighty-Four*. London: Penguin.

Orwell, George. 1937. *The Road to Wigan Pier*. London: Penguin Classics.

Pahl, R.E., & J.T. Winkler. 1975. "The Coming Corporatism." *Challenge* 18, no. 1, 28–35. http://www.jstor.org/stable/40719271.

Pinch, Trevor, and Frank Trocc. 2004. *Analog Days: The Invention and Impact of the Moog Synthesizer*. Cambridge: Harvard University Press.

Plasketes, George. 2013. *Please Allow Me to Introduce Myself: Essays on Debut Albums*. Farnham: Ashgate.

Prendergast, Mark. 2013. *Ambient Century: From Mahler to Moby—The Evolution of Sound in the Electronic Age*. London: Bloomsbury.

Pressing, J. 1992. *Synthesizer Performance and Real-Time Techniques*. Oxford: Oxford University Press.

Reed, Alexander S. 2013. *Assimilate: A Critical History of Industrial Music*. Oxford: Oxford University Press.

Reynolds, Simon. 2009. "One Nation Under a Moog." *Guardian*. October 10. Accessed September 5, 2002. https://www.theguardian.com/music/2009/oct/10/synth-pop-80s-reynolds.

Reynolds, Simon. 2016. *Rip It Up and Start Again*. London: Faber & Faber.

Reynolds, Simon. 2011. *Retromania: Pop Culture's Addiction to Its Own Past*, 1st American ed. London: Faber & Faber.

Reynolds, Simon. 2017. *Shock and Awe: Glam Rock and Its Legacy: From the Seventies to the Twenty-First Century,* paperback ed. London: Faber & Faber.

Rose, N. 2011. "Identity, Genealogy, History." In S. Hall & P. du Gay (eds.), *Questions of Cultural Identity*. SAGE Publications, https://dx.doi.org/10.4135/9781446221907.n8.

Rowthorn, Bob. 1980. "The Politics of the Alternative Economic Strategy." *International Socialism* 2, no. 8 (Spring 1980), 85–94.

Russo, Mary J., & Daniel Noam Warner. 1988. "Rough Music, Futurism, and Post Punk Industrial Noise Bands." *Discourse: Journal for Theoretical Studies in Media and Culture* 10, no. 3.

Savage, Jon. 1988. *Industrial Culture Handbook*. San Francisco: Research Publications.

Shelley, Mary. 1991. *Frankenstein*. Dover: Dover Publications.

Sobchak, V. 1991. "Baudrillard's Obscenity." *Science Fiction Studies* 18, no. 3.

Sommer, Robert. 1969. *Personal Space: The Behavioral Basis of Design*. Hoboken, NJ: Prentice Hall.

Spencer, R. & E. 2000. *Paolozzi: Writings and Interviews*. Oxford: Oxford University Press.

Strange, Steve. 2002. *Blitzed: The Autobiography of Steve Strange*. London: Orion Books.

Stubbs, David. 2018. *Mars by 1980: The Story of Electronic Music*. London: Faber & Faber.

Sutton, Paul. 2016. *Understanding Gary Numan: An Essay on the Machine Quartet (1978–1981)*. Cambridge, UK: Buffalo Books.

Swift, Jonathan. 2003. *Gulliver's Travels*. London: Penguin Classics.

Tambling, Jeremy. 2018. "Baudelaire: The Painter of Modern Life." In J. Tambling (ed.). *The Palgrave Encyclopedia of Urban Literary Studies*, Palgrave Macmillan, Cham. https://doi.org/10.1007/978-3-319-62592-8_83-1.

Toffler, Alvin. 1980. *The First Wave: The Classic Study of Tomorrow*. New York: Bantam Books.

Toop, David. 2018. *Ocean of Sound: Ambient Sound and Radical Listening in the Age of Communication*. London: Serpent's Tail.

Tutti, Cosey Fanni. 2017. *Art Sex Music: Cosey Fanni Tutti*. London: Faber & Faber.

Tzara, Tristan. 1918. *Dada Manifesto*. Publisher unknown. 23rd March.

Virilio, P. 2003. *Art and Fear*. Trans. Julie Rose. London and New York: Continuum.

Ware, Martin. 2022. *Electronically Yours, Volume One*. London: Constable.

Warner, T. 2003. *Pop Music, Technology and Creativity: Trevor Horn and the Digital Revolution*, Farnham: Ashgate.

Wells, H.G. 2013. *When the Sleeper Awakes*. London: Penguin Classics.

Whitney, Carl. 2019. *Hit Factories: A Journey Through the Industrial Cities of British Pop*. London: Weidenfeld & Nicolson.

Wickham-Jones, Mark. 1996. *Economic Strategy and the Labor Party: Politics and Policy-Making, 1970–83*. London: Palgrave Macmillan.

Winkler, J.T. 1975. "Law, State and Economy: The Industry Act 1975." *British Journal of Law and Society* 2, no. 2, 103–28.

Wiener, Norbert. 1965. *Cybernetics or Control and Communication in the Animal and the Machine*. Cambridge: MIT Press.

Williams, Raymond. 1985. *Towards 2000*. London: Penguin.

Wishart, T. 1994. *Audible Design*. London: Orpheus–The Pantomime Press.

Woodstra, Chris, Gerald Brennan, & Allen Schrott (eds.). 2005. *All Music Guide to Classical Music: The Definitive Guide to Classical Music*. Berkeley, CA: Backbeat Books.

Zagorski-Thomas, Simon. 2014. *The Musicology of Record Production*. Cambridge: Cambridge University Press.

# INDEX

# ABOUT THE AUTHOR

**Dr. Neil O'Connor** is an electronic music producer and academic at DMARC (Digital Media Research Centre), Department of Computer Science, University of Limerick, Ireland. Neil has published with Bloomsbury, Taylor & Francis, Routledge, and Cambridge University Press.

Lightning Source UK Ltd.
Milton Keynes UK
UKHW011318230223
417520UK00004B/5

9 781538 165300